INSTRUCTOR'S MANUAL AND TEST BANK
TO ACCOMPANY

CLASSICAL MYTHOLOGY
IMAGES AND INSIGHTS

by
Stephen L. Harris
Gloria Platzner

NINA ROSENSTAND

Mayfield Publishing Company
Mountain View, California
London • Toronto

International Standard Book Number: 1-55934-423-7

Manufactured in the United States of America
10 9 8 7 6 5 4 3 2 1

Mayfield Publishing Company
1280 Villa Street
Mountain View, CA 94041

Contents

PREFACE

This *Instructor's Manual and Test Bank* gives a quick overview of the main points in each chapter of *Classical Mythology* in the form of a numbered summary; it also provides a bank of objective questions and essay questions.

Each chapter in the summary section concludes with two lists of names whenever appropriate. The first list contains the names and functions of the most important mythic characters mentioned in the chapter. The second list contains the names of and basic information about the key sources of classical myths mentioned in the text, either the original storytellers or later mythographers such as translators, revisionists, interpreters, and critics. These names are generally listed in the order in which they appear in the text.

In addition, you will find boxes labeled "Notes" that contain information, generally oriented toward comparative mythology, which your students may find interesting. In order not to detour your students too far from the main topic, the boxes are kept to about one per chapter. Each chapter contains a mention of the primary text selection concluding the chapter, if any; however, since most of the key features of the primary texts are mentioned in the chapter text, there is no summary of the events in the primary texts.

The test bank at the back of the manual contains true/false questions, multiple-choice questions, and essay questions. When the chapter concludes with a primary text selection, the essay questions generally contain excerpts from the selection.

Since objective questions by their very nature tend to mislead the students in their suggestions of incorrect answers, it is a good idea to go over the correct answers with the students after each examination so that the incorrect answers won't be subconsciously remembered as correct ones.

Nina Rosenstand

PART I

CLASS PRESENTATION MATERIALS: A DETAILED OVERVIEW

CHAPTER 1
INTRODUCTION TO THE NATURE OF MYTH

MAIN POINTS

1. The people of Athens (the city was named after the goddess Athene) built the Parthenon temple in her honor. Decorations on the Parthenon depict the birth of Athene, who springs fully armed from Zeus's head. This illustrates a mythical paradox, a male creating life without the participation of a female.

2. Zeus also gave birth to a male child, Dionysus, god of wine and intoxication, who emerged from his father's thigh.

3. Zeus's giving birth to these two children suggests that myth has the power to integrate polar opposites such as rationality and emotionalism.

4. Greek myth shares with religion a conviction that the cosmos has both a physical and a spiritual dimension and that humans participate in both.

5. Myth is as universal as dreams, and, like dreams, it has some connection with everyday reality. Mythic events are subtly grounded in the values of the myth-producing society.

6. The origin of myth may be as old as language itself.

7. The word *myth* (Greek: *mythos*) literally means "utterance" or "something one says."

8. Because myth was an oral tradition, several different versions of a myth developed. It took a long evolutionary process to shape Greek myth as we know it.

9. Herodotus assumed that Greek myth was influenced by Egyptian mythology.

10. Sumerians were the first to record oral myth in written form. The earliest known literary work embodying myth is the *Epic of Gilgamesh.*

11. The *Epic of Gilgamesh* contains an early version of the myth of the global flood; only the hero's ancestor Utnapishtim escapes.

12. The Babylonian creation account, *Enuma Elish,* tells of the young god Marduk, who defeats the older generation of gods and becomes the new universal king.

13. Greek and Mesopotamian mythmakers shared the belief that we inhabit a vertically structured, three-story universe: heaven, earth, and the Underworld.

14. Greek literature reflects the influence of myth. Aristotle defines myth as a plot-structure in a literary work. Other works of literature including mythic elements are the *Homeric Hymns,* the tragic drama, and some lyric poems.

15. Attempts at recording ancient traditions faithfully: The *Library,* attributed (erroneously) to Apollodorus of Athens, contains a large collection of ancient tales. Pausanias's *Guide to Greece* also attempts to record ancient traditions. Plutarch recorded local beliefs and myths of his homeland.

16. The Roman poet Ovid reworked the Greek creation myth to reflect centuries of speculations about the origin of the universe: his work, the *Metamorphoses of the Gods,* contains ironic commentaries about imperial Rome.

17. Virgil's *Aeneid* has been regarded as an attempt to create a heroic past for Rome and to show a paradigm of the ideal Roman citizen, but scholars now doubt whether Virgil intended for his work to support Roman imperialism.

18. Greek storytellers regarded myth as their prehistory: Gods once interacted with humans and then withdrew to Mount Olympus.

19. Some archaeologists believe that myth has some basis in historical fact. Schliemann searched for Troy and Mycenae under the same assumption, and his discovery of these sites may suggest that the siege and fall of Troy is legendary rather than purely mythic.

20. Greek myth originated in the Greek Bronze Age (between about 1600 and 1100 B.C.) in the Mycenaean civilization. The art and architecture of Mycenae were influenced by the older, Minoan civilization.

21. The myth of Theseus slaying the Minotaur is of Minoan origin.

22. About 1100 B.C. the Dorians brought the Mycenaean civilization to an end, plunging Greece into the Dark Ages, which lasted for several hundred years. Mycenaean refugees settled and prospered along the coast of Ionia in what is now Western Turkey, where a Greek renaissance emerged.

23. Sagas are stories about a particular city or family, usually about a military aristocracy, while folktales tell about the experiences of the common folk and usually do not include myth's preoccupation with the struggles of the human spirit. Some works based on myth may contain elements of folklore.

24. In the hands of the great poets, Greek myths acquire a focus on humanistic values, placing human consciousness in the center of the universe. Protagoras declared, "Man is the measure of all things."

25. The anthropomorphism of Greek myths, portraying the Gods as human-like, distinguishes Greek art and literature; in contrast, Egyptian mythology represented gods in animal form.

26. Greek myth emphasizes competitiveness and individualism. A character embodying individualism is Achilles; a tradition embodying competitiveness is the Olympic Games. The myths continually express the idea that the obsessive quest for preeminence is a noble goal, but it exacts a terrible cost—an element in the lives of the Greek gods as well as in the lives of the Greek heroes.

KEY NAMES OF MYTHOLOGICAL CHARACTERS MENTIONED

Athene, Zeus's daughter and goddess of wisdom and military victory; protector of the city of Athens

Zeus, king of heaven

Dionysus, son of Zeus, god of wine and ecstasy

Gilgamesh, Sumerian king of Uruk

Marduk, a young male Babylonian deity

Theseus, a Greek hero slaying the Minotaur in Crete

Minotaur, a creature with a bull's head and a human body

Achilles, the hero of Homer's *Iliad,* a Greek warrior at the battle of Troy

KEY NAMES ASSOCIATED WITH THE TELLING/CRITICISM OF MYTHS

Homer, Greek poet (ninth century B.C.)

Hesiod, Greek mythographer (eighth century B.C.)

Herodotus, Greek historian (fifth century B.C.)

Apollodorus of Athens, Greek mythographer (c. 140 B.C.)

Pausanias, Roman historian (second century A.D.)

Plutarch, Greek biographer (c. A.D. 46–c. 120)

Virgil, Roman poet (70–19 B.C.)

Ovid, Roman poet (43 B.C.–17 A.D.)

CHAPTER 2
WAYS OF INTERPRETING MYTH

MAIN POINTS

1. Architectural features of the Parthenon show victories of civilization over savagery, including Athene's triumphs, and portray the gods as calm and relaxed. In contrast, earthly scenes depict conflicts.

2. The Parthenon scenes, together with decorations on Greek sanctuaries, illustrate the close connection between myth and Greek society by evoking the mythic past and suggesting the continuing patronage of the gods.

3. Even though myth played the role of ancient history and theology, the Greek myths did not have the binding authority of scripture. The Greeks considered foreign deities as analogous to their own gods.

4. The Greek philosophical movement (after the sixth century B.C.) introduced some skepticism, but was mainly used to rationalize certain aspects of Greek myth.

5. Euripides interprets the myth of the birth of Dionysus from Zeus's thigh as an allegory, functioning through metaphor and figurative language.

6. Theagenes of Rhegion is reported to have stated that when Homer tells of gods fighting each other, he is really creating allegories about natural processes in which the elements (hot, dry, wet, cold) are in perpetual conflict. Likewise, the gods can signify human dispositions.

7. Anaxagoras interpreted Homeric hymn as exposing the evil results of unethical conduct and promoting virtue.

8. Xenophanes of Colophon complained about the gods' lack of moral values; Socrates and Plato found the Homeric myths morally offensive, even though Plato himself used myths to illustrate his philosophical worldview (the theory of Forms).

NOTE: Some of Plato's best-known myths or fables include the Myth (Allegory) of the Cave and the Myth of Er, both from the *Republic,* and the Myth of the Charioteer, from *Phaedrus.* The term *myth* is used here to signify a symbolic story rather than a traditional narrative about gods and heroes. See chapter 19.

---

9. Euhemerus of Messene claimed to have found written evidence that the Greek gods were once mortal, ancient kings. This theory is now known as Euhemerism.

10. In spite of criticism, myth remained a cultural factor until the legitimization of Christianity in the fourth century A.D. Classical myth was banned from Western culture through the Middle Ages; the European Renaissance reintroduced myth to the world of art and literature. The Enlightenment inspired new, scholarly interest in the interpretation of myth.

11. Mythology has two general meanings: (1) a set or system of myths and (2) a methodological analysis of myths.

12. Using a methodological analyses of myths, scholars have attempted to find a unifying element behind the varied components of myth.

13. Scholarly theories of myth generally fall into one of two groups: those that assume an external basis of myth, and those that see mythmaking as an expression of the human mind.

14. The nature myth theory is externalistic: myth is a reaction to the awe-inspiring powers of physical nature—the cycles of day and night, summer and winter, plant life and death.

15. Often the gods serve as personification of meteorological forces and astronomical functions or objects.

16. The nature myth theory, advocated in the nineteenth century, interpreted myths allegorically to fit the theory. Proponent: F. Max Müller.

17. Criticism: The nature myth theory fails to account for the full content of most myths.

18. The theory of ritual is externalistic: myths are the by-product of ritual enactments, invented to explain the ceremonies. Proponent: Sir James Frazer.

19. Criticism: The ritual theory does not explain why rituals develop in the first place.

20. The charter theory is externalistic: myths are narratives that supply the rationale for some ritual or custom in order to help maintain social stability. Proponent: Bronislaw Malinowski.

21. Example: Hesiod explains why the Greeks sacrifice the least desirable parts of animals to the gods; tradition established through trickery.

22. Criticism: The charter theory fails to explain why human welfare is favored over divine prerogative.

23. The etiological theory is externalistic: (1) Myth is primitive science, attempting to explain natural phenomena. (2) Myth can also give theological or metaphysical interpretations of the human condition.

24. Example: Hesiod explains why the human possession of fire led to alienation between men and gods.

25. Criticism: Many myths and heroic tales have little to do with etiology.

26. Freudian theory is a psychological theory, emphasizing the internal character of myth: like dreams, myths allow humans to violate taboos safely through displacement, as a form of wish fulfillment. Proponent: Sigmund Freud.

27. Freud divides the mind into three basic components—the *id,* the *ego,* and the *superego*—which in some ways mirror the Greek tripartite universe of Underworld, the earth, and the realm of the gods.

NOTE: Freud's theory of the tripartite psyche also resembles, to a certain degree, Plato's view of the human psyche. For Plato, the human mind consists of reason, willpower (passion), and appetites (desires). The Myth of the Charioteer in *Phaedrus* compares reason to a charioteer, and willpower and appetites to his two horses. While the appetites can be compared to Freud's category of the *id,* there is one important difference: for Freud the *id* is unconscious and inaccessible to the conscious mind, whereas for Plato the appetites are part of the conscious mind. See chapter 19.

---

28. Example: The story of Oedipus, who kills his father and marries his mother.

29. Advantage of Freudian theory: it helps explain tragic myths through insight into domestic psychodrama.

30. Criticism: Greek male hostility toward females may have ancient cultural roots.

31. The theory of archetypes is psychological: myths, like dreams, contain universal archetypes springing from the collective unconscious. Proponent: Carl Jung.

32. Example: The male mind contains a female component, the anima, while the female mind has a male component, the animus. In a healthy psyche, the anima and the animus have a harmonious relationship.

33. Example: The shadow, Jung's term for unacknowledged negative elements of the psyche, contains repressed or undervalued aspects of the personality.

34. Scholars associated with psychological analysis of myth: Joseph Campbell, Ernst Cassirer, Mircea Eliade, and Victor Turner. Myth and ritual are interpreted as structuring the human world and easing transitions in life.

35. The theory of structuralism views myth as a reflection of the mind's binary organization. Humans project a binary significance onto experience, dividing everything into polar opposites. Myth deals with and reconciles these opposites. Proponent: Claude Lévi-Strauss.

36. Scholars associated with the structural theory of myth: Jean-Pierre Vernant and Pierre Vidal-Nanquet.

37. Criticism: Not all myths present a quantitative division of opposites.

38. The approach of this text is to use a variety of methodologies rather than to force myth into one theoretical mold. Certain myths invite a certain method of interpretation, and others don't.

KEY NAMES OF MYTHOLOGICAL CHARACTERS MENTIONED

Athene

Apollo, god of health, mental discipline, and artistic creativity

Artemis, Apollo's twin sister, patron of wildlife and the hunt

Poseidon, Zeus's brother, lord of the sea and earthquakes

Ares, god of bloodshed and war

Demeter, sister of Zeus and Poseidon, goddess of earth's fertility

Hermes, trickster god of thieves, gamblers, and businessmen

Dionysus

Oedipus, king of Thebes, who killed his father and married his mother

KEY NAMES ASSOCIATED WITH THE TELLING/CRITICISM OF MYTHS

Phidias, Athenian sculptor (c. 500–c. 432 B.C.)

Euripides, Greek tragic dramatist (480–406 B.C.)

Theagenes of Rhegion (c. 525 B.C.)

Anaxagoras, Greek philosopher (500–428 B.C.)

Xenophanes of Colophon, Greek philosopher (sixth century B.C.)

Socrates, Greek philosopher (c. 469–399 B.C.)

Plato, Greek philosopher (c. 427–349 B.C.)

Euhemerus of Messene, Sicilian philosopher (fourth century B.C.)

F. Max Müller, German philologist (1823–1900)

Sir James Frazer, English anthropologist (1854–1941)

Bronislaw Malinowski, Polish anthropologist (1884–1942)

Sigmund Freud, Austrian psychoanalyst (1856–1939)

Carl Jung, Swiss analytical psychologist (1875–1961)

Claude Lévi-Strauss, French anthropologist (1908–)

CHAPTER 3

IN THE BEGINNING: HESIOD'S *THEOGONY*

MAIN POINTS

1. Greek poets promoted a mythic conception of the universe rather than a scientific one, based partly on ancient Near Eastern models and partly on commonsensical observations of their environment.

2. According to the Greeks, the earth is a flat, circular disc with mountains touching the bowl of the sky; the land is surrounded by ocean, and below lies the Underworld, the land of the dead.

3. This model of heaven, earth, and the Underworld is called a cosmos. The subject of Hesiod's *Theogony* (the origin of the gods) is both a cosmogony (origin of the universe) and a cosmology (the nature and purpose of the universe).

4. Hesiod begins with Chaos and then tells of Gaea, Tartarus, and Eros springing into existence independently. A primary focus of the *Theogony* is divine genealogy.

5. Hesiod's interest in conflict may have an autobiographical origin: a life of poverty and hard work and conflicts with his brother.

6. Hesiod ascribed the origin of his inspiration to the Muses, the nine daughters of Zeus and Mnemosyne.

7. *Theogony* contains much traditional material inherited from Mesopotamia such as the generational shift of the divine rulers, the slaying of the monster, and the castration theme.

8. Zeus is the grandson of Gaea and her firstborn son, Uranus. Gaea's and Uranus's children are the Titans, including Cronus and Rhea, Zeus's parents.

> **NOTE:** The genealogy of the Olympian family is not unlike the genealogy of the Aesir, the Norse family of gods. Like Zeus, Odin—the ruler of the gods—is a third-generation divinity. Odin is the son of Borr and the grandson of the first proto-human, Bure, a handsome creature born from the Scandinavian rocks. Odin and his two brothers, Vile and Ve, create the world out of the slain giant Ymir, and proceed to create man and woman from two trees.

9. The castration of Uranus: Gaea resents Uranus for not allowing her to give birth to the children she is carrying. With a sickle made by Gaea, her son Cronus severs his father's genitals and throws them into the sea.

10. From the phallic blood spilled onto the earth a race of giants is created along with the Furies, female spirits. The phallus itself, mixing with semen and foam, is transformed into Aphrodite rising from the sea.

11. The ambiguity of the story: It brings Zeus closer to being the reigning god, but it also introduces hatred and revenge. Also, the act of love can inspire acts of violent aggression along with joy and beauty.

12. Cronus attempts to avoid Uranus's fate by devouring his children.

NOTE: Many scholars have traditionally assumed that just as the name Uranus has a literal meaning ("starry sky"), so does the name Cronus (Kronos), since it is similar to the Greek word for "time," *chronos*. This has led to the famous symbolic interpretation that Time devours his children—i.e., all children born of time (including human beings) will, in the end, be devoured by time and die. However, other scholars believe that there is no etymological justification for this interpretation.

---

13. Approaches to the castration myth from several theories of myth:
    a. A fragment of historical memory: the overthrowing of tribal leaders by strong sons, perhaps involving ritual castration of the deposed patriarch.
    b. A feminist interpretation: a remnant of a matriarchal rite where the primal goddess's consort was killed and perhaps eaten as part of a fertility ritual.
    c. An etiological theory: an explanation of the psychological affinity between love and hate, of the division between masculine and feminine principles, and of why the "starry sky" is remote.
    d. A Freudian theory: a domestic psychodrama between father, son, and mother.

14. The birth of Athene: Zeus marries his first wife, Metis. Worried that he may have a son strong enough to overthrow him, Zeus swallows the pregnant Metis; by assimilating her, he is able to give birth to Athene.

15. Approaches to the myth of Athene's birth from several theories:
    a. A nature myth: human thought takes place in the brain.
    b. The etiological function: a shift from matriarchal to patriarchal rule.
    c. The charter function: the validation of patriarchy and a marriage in which the man subdues the woman.
    d. A Jungian interpretation: a representation of the archetypal union of animus and anima.
    e. A psychoanalytical interpretation: the male fear of the castrating female.
    f. A Freudian interpretation: Zeus reenacts the Oedipal fear of and competition with the father, preventing future rivalry by incorporating all threats within his body.
    g. A rite of passage: Zeus progresses from an inexperienced warrior to a mature ruler.
    h. A structuralist interpretation: reconciliation of natural, instinctual, physical component (Zeus) with rational intellect (Metis).

16. Athene is the goddess of wisdom, but also the goddess of victory in war. These qualities are needed to save Zeus from his potential undoing.

17. Hera, Zeus's sister and last wife, is generally represented as his rival for power and may have been worshipped independently prior to the advent of patriarchal religion.

18. Hera gives birth (without male assistance) to Hephaestus, who becomes his mother's political support.

19. Gaea, representing the feminine principle, makes Zeus confront her child, the monster Typhoeus.

20. One theory is that Typhoeus may be a patriarchal perversion of the Great Goddess's wise serpent.

NOTE: The same theory of patriarchal perversion has been advanced in connection with the model for the story of Zeus and the monster, the Babylonian story of Marduk defeating Tiamat. The giant snake-monster Tiamat is herself female and a creator-goddess in the original story of *Enuma Elish,* thus bringing the theme closer to its supposed origin of the snake-monster in an ancient goddess religion. See chapter 6.

---

21. The battle between Zeus and Typhoeus may contain a faint memory of a geological catastrophe such as a volcanic eruption.

22. Support for the theory: One etiological tradition states that Zeus defeated Typhoeus by burying him beneath Mount Etna, the largest and most active volcano in Europe.

23. Hesiod's worldview is inherently contradictory: proliferation of life is also marked by acts of violence. Zeus's triumph is depicted as good; however, Hesiod was pessimistic about human social and moral values.

PRIMARY TEXT SELECTION: Hesiod, *Theogony*

KEY NAMES OF MYTHOLOGICAL CHARACTERS MENTIONED

Gaea, the earth and the primordial mother

Eros, god of procreative love

Mnemosyne, a personification of memory

The Muses:
>   Calliope (epic poetry), Clio (history), Polyhymnia (mime), Melpomone (tragedy), Thalia (comedy), Erato (lyric choral poetry), Euterpe (the flute), Terpsichore (light verse and dance), Urania (astronomy)

Uranus, firstborn son of Gaea

Titans, a race of giants born to Uranus and Gaea

Cronus, the Titan leader, Zeus's father

Rhea, Cronus's sister–wife, Zeus's mother

Aphrodite, goddess of love, beauty, and sexual desire

Metis, Zeus's first wife, swallowed by Zeus

Hera, Zeus's sister and last wife

Hephaestus, Hera's son, disabled from birth or from an accident

Typhoeus, a reptilian monster, Gaea's youngest son with Tartarus; a monster/an abyss; defeated by Zeus in battle

KEY NAMES ASSOCIATED WITH THE TELLING/CRITICISM OF MYTHS

Hesiod, Greek mythographer (eighth century B.C.)

CHAPTER 4

THE WORLD IN DECLINE:
ALIENATION OF THE HUMAN AND DIVINE

MAIN POINTS

1. The ambiguity of Hesiod's creation account also exists in his view of human history: with Zeus as the new leader of the gods, humans are worse off than before.

2. When Prometheus steals fire from the gods and gives it to humans, Zeus chains him to a mountain crag, where an eagle feasts on his liver.

3. To punish men for accepting Prometheus's gift, Zeus has Hephaestus make the first woman, Pandora. Before Pandora, men mingled with the gods; after her appearance, the gods withdraw from the world of mortals.

4. Here Hesiod emphasizes a connection between food, sacrifice, fire, cooking, and woman.

5. The Greek and Judeo-Christian traditions agree on seeing woman as the catalyst of humanity's historical decline.

6. Pandora brings a jar from which she releases all evils, ending the Golden Age. She serves the same mythic function as Eve in Genesis.

7. In Genesis, a serpent persuades Eve to eat the forbidden fruit, which gives knowledge of good and evil.

8. The forbidden fruit is the biblical counterpart of the Promethean fire: enlightenment and cultural separation from nature.

9. In both the Bible and Greek myth, humanity pays a price for knowledge: loss of innocence, loss of peace, and loss of paradise.

10. Pandora may have been an earth goddess, the "Giver of All."

11. Other versions of the Pandora myth claim that the jar contains blessings, which she inadvertently lets out; only Hope is caught before it can escape.

12. A more positive view of woman's mythic role: The *Epic of Gilgamesh* tells of Enkidu, the savage male, who is civilized through a sexual relationship with a priestess of the goddess Ishtar.

13. Greek mythology is essentially male and typically views female intelligence as a threat to male security.

14. Hesiod saw the cosmos permeated with two forms of Strife: mindless aggression and healthy competition.

15. Hesiod's *Works and Days* divides human history into five ages, containing no account of man's creation.

16. During the first period, the Age of Gold, Cronus ruled the world. Humans lived in complete freedom and in company with the gods. Their bodies died after a long, vigorous life, but their spirits remained alive.

17. The Age of Silver, a lesser age, is characterized by opposites: people had a childhood of a hundred years, but died soon after maturation through violence. Zeus ordered their extinction because they refused to worship their creators.

18. During the Age of Bronze, men were created by Zeus from ash trees and pursued mindless, violent conflicts. In the end they annihilated each other.

NOTE: The theme of the ash tree finds a parallel in Nordic mythology, which may have an ancient, Indo-European root in common with Greek myth: the first man and woman are created from trees by Odin and his brothers, and in the middle of the world grows the world tree Yggdrasil, a mighty ash tree with roots in the Underworld and branches reaching to the home of the gods; humans live in the middle on its lower branches, in Midgaard.

---

19. The Age of Heroes: Probably inserted into an older tradition, this age has no corresponding metal and does not signify a steady decline. The great heroes of the siege of Troy and other battles live and die during this epoch; after death they are allowed to live in a remote paradise.

20. The biblical Book of Daniel has a similar account of four historical ages symbolized by a huge statue composed of four different metals.

21. The Age of Iron, the time of Hesiod himself, is brutal and harsh and will end when Zeus wipes out the present generation. The End is near when even newborns have gray hair and social order disappears.

22. Hesiod's view of history is apocalyptic: an end of the world, preceded by four mass extinctions. There is no way to escape the designs of Zeus.

23. Although not mentioned by Hesiod, the myth of the global flood is an important element in Greek mythology. Deucalion and Pyrrha survive the flood in an ark and, when the waters have subsided, repopulate the earth by throwing stones over their shoulders which become men and women.

KEY NAMES OF MYTHOLOGICAL CHARACTERS MENTIONED

Cronus, son of Uranus, father of Zeus

Prometheus, a Titan

Pandora, the first woman in the Greek tradition

Eve, the first woman in the Judeo-Christian tradition

Adam, the first man in the Judeo-Christian tradition

Yahwe, God of the Judeo-Christian tradition

Epimetheus, Prometheus's brother

Enkidu, the savage man, Gilgamesh's friend

Gilgamesh, the Sumerian king of Uruk

Ishtar, the Great Goddess of Sumerian tradition

Deucalion, Prometheus's son, survivor of the flood

Pyrrha, Deucalion's wife, survivor of the global flood

KEY NAMES ASSOCIATED WITH THE TELLING/CRITICISM OF MYTHS

Hesiod (eighth century B.C.)

Apollodorus (c. 140 B.C.)

Ovid (43 B.C.–17 A.D.)

Aeschylus, Greek tragic dramatist (525–456 B.C.)

CHAPTER 5

THE OLYMPIAN FAMILY OF ZEUS

MAIN POINTS

1. Herodotus claims that Homer and Hesiod defined the characters of the gods fairly recently compared to the antiquity of Egypt.

2. According to Homer, Zeus and his two brothers divided the world by casting lots. Zeus received the sky, Poseidon the sea, and Hades the Underworld.

3. The children of Cronus and Rhea (Zeus, Poseidon, Hades, Hera, Demeter, and Hestia) are depicted as having physically mature, perfect human forms.

4. Zeus: King of Heaven, champion of justice, sworn oaths, and lawful order.

NOTE: There is linguistic evidence that many of the European, Middle Eastern, and Indian cultures share a common ancestral culture. The ancient, Proto-Indo-European people whose territories have not been established firmly because of conflicting archaeological and linguistic evidence, but who may have occupied areas between the Danube and the Volga rivers, north of the Caucasus mountain range, have supplied common words to Indo-European languages all the way from Ireland to Chinese Turkestan. The Proto-Indo-European words for "one-two-three" are "oinos-duwo-treyes"; "brother" is "bhrater," "sky" is "dyeus," and "father" is "pater." From this last constellation of words (sky-father) come the names of Zeus and Jupiter. However, linguists warn that we can't assume that gods have had the same role in the ancient Indo-European culture as they had later in the Mediterranean area. Today, English and Spanish are the most common Indo-European languages in the world; the most ancient Indo-European language still spoken is thought to be Romany, the language of the Gypsies.

---

5. It is unclear whether Zeus is in control of Fate or if Fate is superior to the gods.

6. Hesiod implies Zeus's control by making him the father of the Moirae, the three sisters who spin and weave the patterns controlling mortal lives.

7. Zeus also sires Lawfulness (Eunomia), Justice (Dike), and Peace (Eirene), indicating that the cosmos is held in relative harmony by him.

8. The paradoxical nature of Zeus's character: patriarch of Heaven, with uncontrollable sexual appetite. Zeus's lust is both his "shadow" and his will to dominate. His desire is often treated humorously; he frequently assumes the form of an animal when pursuing a new lover.

9. Poseidon's symbol is the trident, with which he generates huge waves. Poseidon represents the brutal power of nature: the restless sea, the shaking earth, and the virility of certain land animals.

10. Hades rules the Underworld with his wife, Persephone, and wears a cap of invisibility. He is also associated with the gems and minerals of the earth.

11. Hera, Zeus's wife and elder sister, is the patron of married life; her symbol is the peacock; her offspring are Hephaestus, Ares, Eileithyia, and Hebe.

12. Demeter represents the life-giving power of earth's soil. A manifestation of the Great Goddess, she is the giver of grain.

13. When Persephone, her daughter, is kidnapped by Hades, Demeter grieves for her to the extent that plants wither and die. Persephone, who must stay for part of the year with Hades, represents the cycle of growth, death, and rebirth.

14. Athene, the patron of wisdom and military victory, also supervises women's crafts. Otherwise self-disciplined, one myth shows her engaging in a beauty competition with Hera and Aphrodite which results in the Trojan war.

15. Athene is loyal to the heroes of intelligence and resourcefulness, but cruel to humans who offend her.

16. Apollo, son of Zeus and Leto, is the giver of rational harmony and has precognition. He established the Delphic Oracle.

17. In late myths, Apollo takes over the function as sun-god; in addition he is the protector of the muses and bringer of sickness by way of arrows. His son Asclepius, the first physician, represents his healing aspect.

18. Artemis, Apollo's twin sister, is the patron of midwifery and childbirth but is also a virgin who guards her privacy.

19. Artemis is, in addition, patron of the hunt and protector of wild animals. She is often identified with the moon. In Asia Minor the Greeks associated Artemis with fertility.

20. Hermes, son of Zeus, is Zeus's personal messenger, depicted with winged heels. Hermes invents the lyre and the panpipes, which Apollo takes over in exchange for cattle and the caduceus, a rod entwined by two serpents and topped by wings, the symbol of the physician's art.

21. Hermes is also guide of souls on their way to the Underworld. The patron of travelers, traders, merchants, highwaymen, thieves, and gamblers, he is also associated with dreams and magic.

22. Hephaestus, Hera's son, is a gifted craftsman married to Aphrodite, who is unfaithful to him.

23. Aphrodite is a personification of human sexuality.

24. Eros is the masculine aspect of Aphrodite and, according to Homer, her son by Ares.

25. Ares is the god of war in its aspect of cruelty and violence.

26. Dionysus, god of wine, intoxication, and ecstasy, is the only major god who is born human. He is the patron of the tragic drama.

27. Minor deities control specific landforms or areas; they include the naiads and the dryads.

28. Pan, the shape of a satyr, is a personification of wild nature; he produces enchanting music but also can strike the human heart with fear (panic).

NOTE: The god Pan is, in late Greek tradition, a minor deity, but the worship of Pan-type dieties such as the Fauns seems to have been widespread; the mythologist Sir James Frazer mentions that Pan was known in Arcadia as the Lord of the Woods and was considered a woodland diety. According to Frazer, other goat-formed spirits of the woods can be found in Russian folklore, where the *Ljeschie* are believed to appear partly in human shape, but with the horns, ears, and legs of a goat. The theme of the Pan-type spirit of the woods may have continued with characters in human form such as the Green Man of the Forest in later European tradition, the Shakespearean character of Puck, the quasi-historical Robin Hood, and the children's trickster playmate Peter Pan.

---

29. Greek skeptics such as Xenophanes viewed the Greek gods as relative to the society that created them. According to Xenophanes, if a horse or a lion had gods, they would look like horses and lions.

30. Later Greek thinkers attempted to rationalize the myths, suggesting that the gods were originally heroes who had been deified by posterity.

NOTE: This tradition, Euhemerism, is presented in chapter 2.

---

31. Another approach was that of Xenophanes himself, who believed that the gods are aspects of a single, unknown deity.

KEY NAMES OF MYTHOLOGICAL CHARACTERS MENTIONED

Zeus (Roman: Jupiter)

Cronus (Roman: Saturn)

Demeter (Roman: Ceres)

Hestia, the virgin goddess caring for the Olympian hearth (Roman: Vesta)

Poseidon (Roman: Neptune)

Hades (Roman: Pluto, Dis)

Persephone (Roman: Proserpina)

Hera (Roman: Juno)

Hephaestus, the lame smith, Hera's son (Roman: Vulcanus)

Ares (Roman: Mars)

Eileithyia, goddess of childbirth (Roman: Lucina)

Hebe, a personification of youth (Roman: Juventas)

Athene (Roman: Minerva)

Phoebus Apollo (Roman: Phoebus Apollo)

Leto, Apollo's mother, daughter of Titans

Asclepius, Apollo's son, the first physician

Artemis (Roman: Diana)

Hermes (Roman: Mercurius)

Aphrodite (Roman: Venus)

Eros, the masculine aspect of sexuality, Aphrodite's son according to Homer (Roman: Cupido)

Dionysus (Roman: Liber)

Pan, the personification of wild nature (Roman: Faunus)

KEY NAMES ASSOCIATED WITH THE TELLING/CRITICISM OF MYTHS

Herodotus (fifth century B.C.)

Homer (ninth century B.C.)

Hesiod (eighth century B.C.)

Xenophanes (sixth century B.C.)

Plato (c. 427–347 B.C.)

CHAPTER 6

THE GREAT GODDESS AND THE GODDESSES: THE DIVINE WOMAN IN GREEK MYTHOLOGY

MAIN POINTS

1. Feminist scholars and archaeologists have demonstrated that from the Paleolithic through the Bronze Age there is evidence of Goddess worship.

2. The Great Goddess occurs in myth systems worldwide. Greek myths: Gaea and Demeter; Roman myths: Ceres and Terra Mater; Egyptian myths: Isis; Sumerian myths: Inanna; Babylonian myths: Ishtar; Norse myths: Nerthus.

3. Before the male's role in procreation was understood, the creative powers of the female were attributes of the Great Goddess, who is associated with three functions—as the source of life, of death, and of rebirth.

4. The Great Goddess's triple nature is repeated in the patterns of heaven-earth-Underworld and maiden-mother-old woman.

5. When agriculture was developed, the Goddess was identified as a grain or earth goddess, responsible for the annual agricultural cycle.

6. One of the Goddess's symbols is the serpent, associated with the Underworld and with rebirth through the shedding of its skin. A related symbol is the World Tree, often depicted with a serpent twined around the trunk.

7. Other common Goddess symbols: the moon, vessels, birds, the sow, the cow.

8. The division of the three aspects of the Goddess into separate functions may in part reflect the invasion of Europe by martial, patriarchal Indo-European cultures worshipping sky gods. The Goddess is absorbed into forms not threatening to the sky gods, such as virgin-wife-mistress.

9. Patriarchy creates a new archetype, the hero, focusing on individual achievement and not on cyclical processes. Thus death becomes final.

10. Patriarchy transforms the positive attributes of the Great Goddess into negative attributes. Example: the snake becomes a dragon.

11. The Great Goddess in Greek myth is Gaea, the parthenogenic source of the universe. A transition figure, she compromises with the masculine principle by mating with Uranus to produce offspring.

12. The castration and overthrow of Uranus may be a form of *sparagmos,* the ritual dismemberment and eating of the male god or consort to ensure new life.

13. The violence against Uranus may reflect Oedipal envy, but from a feminine viewpoint it perpetuates the power of the goddess.

14. Zeus's battle with the dragon Typhoeus is a version of the battle with the World Serpent who incorporates the female archetype.

NOTE: Battles between sky gods and world serpents are frequent mythic themes; in addition to Zeus's battle with Typhoeus, Greek tradition contains the stories of Apollo and the dragon Python (see chapter 7) and Cadmus and the dragon (see chapter 18). A parallel in Sumerian tradition is the battle between Marduk and the creator-goddess Tiamat; a Scandinavian parallel is the battle between Thor and the Midgaard worm, the World Serpent of the Norse myths (Thor does not succeed in slaying the worm, however, until the final days of the world, the Ragnarok; seconds after killing the worm, he perishes from his wounds). Another famous battle between hero and snake is told by the British tradition where Beowulf slays not only a female monster (Grendel's mother) but also a treasure-guarding dragon, and by the Norse tradition where Sigurd slays the treasure-guarding, and virgin-guarding, serpent Fafnir. The theme of the hero slaying the dragon remains strong in Western culture where it not only is familiar through the medieval image of St. George and the dragon but also persists in films and literature of today: from *Moby Dick* (updated in the shape of the shark in *Jaws*) to the alien mother-monster in *Aliens 2* (slain by a female hero for a change).

---

15. The Great Goddess in Greek myth is, in her death-wielding aspect, transformed into an old hag, such as the Gorgon, or into a witch, such as Hecate. The maid and mother aspects are reinvoked in forms subordinate to Zeus: Athene, Hera, and Aphrodite.

16. Demeter has all the functions of the Great Goddess except the capacity for parthenogenesis: Zeus is Persephone's father.

17. As a nature myth, the story of Persephone represents the seed, planted underground and sprouting in the spring.

18. As an etiological myth, the story explains why there are seasons.

19. As a charter myth, the story sets up social practices, from the Eleusinian Mysteries to the setting of a place at the table in honor of Demeter.

20. The Eleusinian Mysteries were a nine-day event celebrated each September and October in Eleusis outside of Athens. Not much information is available about them because of their nature as a mystery religion for initiates. Rituals may have included a hieros gamos (sacred marriage) and an epiphany of the goddess showing a seed of grain symbolizing rebirth.

21. The ritual may have incorporated elements from the worship of Dionysus during his festival, since he and Demeter/Persephone share some attributes.

22. The Thesmophoria was a sowing ritual, practiced by women only, that involved placing sacrificed pigs in a gully with snakes, pine cones, and cakes in phallic shapes. After three days, women would descend into the pit and retrieve the material, which would then be mixed with seeds for next year's crop.

23. There is a reconciliation of the Persephone myth with patriarchy through the mediation of Zeus, who arranges the compromise between Hades and Demeter for sharing Persephone.

24. The Persephone myth also reconciles the Great Goddess with patriarchy through the institution of marriage. Persephone's marriage is presented as legal rape and brings about her symbolic death and descent to the Underworld.

25. Demeter embodies the triple aspect of the goddess as mother, grain goddess, and goddess of the mysteries, as well as mother (Demeter), the maiden (Persephone), and the older woman (Hecate). Persephone has a triple aspect symbolized by Athene, Artemis, and Persephone herself.

26. The Persephone myth upholds female values: self-fulfillment in terms of continuity of the generations and the bond between mother and daughter, as opposed to the masculine archetypal experience of individuality, and hostility between father and son.

27. The female experiences renewal through sexuality by giving birth; Demeter becomes her daughter, and Persephone becomes her mother.

28. The Persephone myth presents the female principle as a source of agriculture through Demeter teaching the secrets of life to Triptolemus.

29. Demeter presents an alternative story of civilization, compared to the myth of Prometheus: by giving humans fire (and thus civilization, including weapons), Prometheus sets them free from the gods but creates antagonism between men and gods; Demeter's gift emphasizes bonding and reconciliation.

30. The Persephone myth explores the psychology of the individual woman's life cycles, both as mother and as daughter.

31. Persephone goes through the process of sexual maturation and marriage; the pomegranate symbolizes sexual experience but may also be an emblem of menstruation. Persephone eating the pomegranate may be compared to Eve eating the fruit of the Tree of Knowledge.

32. As Persephone is transformed by the experience, so is Hades: from rapist and abductor to husband.

33. Athene is the wisdom aspect of the Great Goddess; because of her birth from the head of Zeus, she combines the male archetype with the domestic bonds of the female.

34. Hera retains the parthenogenic powers of the Great Goddess and may be related to both the Cretan snake goddess and the cow. Through her Zeus becomes a god of family love.

35. Aphrodite, as an embodiment of Eros, was initially a powerful creative force, but under the patriarchy of the Greek myth she is transformed to a lesser figure of a flirt or a mistress.

36. Ancient archetypal patterns are present in Aphrodite: her relationship with Ares signifies her dual role as goddess of love and war. Similar to other goddess-consort relationships (Isis and Osiris, Ishtar and Tammuz), Aphrodite's love for Adonis involves resurrection through love.

NOTE: The theme of the Goddess going all the way to the Underworld to search for her dead lover in order to bring him back is widespread in the ancient world. Although she does not go to the Underworld, Isis searches all over Egypt to find her dead husband, Osiris. Ishtar, powerful as she is, is only partially successful in buying her dead young lover, Tammuz, back from the land of the dead. Inanna goes to rescue her lover, Dumuzi. Demeter's search for Persephone is of course a related theme, although there is an important difference: Demeter is looking for her daughter, in effect her alter ego, not her lover. A Greek variation of the theme places the male in the role of the searcher going to the Underworld: Orpheus searches for his dead wife, Eurydice, in the land of the dead and almost manages to bring her back (see chapters 8 and 9). The mythic theme is known in other cultures as well: among the Native American Modocs of the Pacific Coast the culture hero Kumokum travels to the land of the dead to fetch back his beloved daughter but fails like Orpheus, and in an African myth a young hero goes to the Underworld to free the young girl Wanjiru, who was sacrificed by her family. Of all these stories, only the story of Wanjiru has a completely successful ending: Wanjiru is saved, she and the warrior get married, and her family is ashamed for having sacrificed her.

---

37. Artemis inherits the chthonic aspect of the goddess, being associated with the moon and Hecate. She is the guardian of women's mysteries, representing the power of instinct by being the guardian of wild animals.

38. Hecate is connected to the Underworld and has powers of earth and sea. She has come to represent the death-giving aspect of the goddess and has become associated with fear. She is identified as a witch or an older woman.

39. The *Homeric Hymn to Demeter,* probably dating from the seventh century B.C., tells about the abduction of Persephone; it also tells the story of Demeter's caring for the child Demophon and her attempt to make him immortal.

40. The story of Demophon serves as a charter myth for the mystery and functions as a way of achieving symbolic immortality through communion with Demeter.

KEY NAMES OF MYTHOLOGICAL CHARACTERS MENTIONED

(Reflecting the theme of this chapter, the male gods are identified below in terms of their relation to the goddesses, to break the patriarchal pattern of identifying the goddesses in relation to the male gods.)

Gaea, the parthenogenic earth goddess

Uranus, her son and spouse

Zeus, Hera's husband and Demeter's brother

Typhoeus, Gaea's offspring, a monster slain by Zeus

The Gorgons, three sister witches; best known is Medusa

Hecate, the death-giving aspect of the Goddess

Athene

Hera

Aphrodite

Demeter

Persephone (Kore)

Dionysus, the son of Semele

Hades, Persephone's husband

Artemis

Triptolemus, the holy child and first farmer of the Eleusinian myth

Prometheus, the Titan who stole fire from the gods and gave it to humans

Adonis, Aphrodite's lover

Demophon, the child in Demeter's care

CHAPTER 7

IN TOUCH WITH THE GODS:
APOLLO'S ORACLE AT DELPHI

MAIN POINTS

1. The geographical features of Delphi on Mount Parnassus included a theater, a stadium, and the temple.

2. Delphi's reputation reached its peak between the seventh and fifth centuries B.C. The facade of the temple was inscribed with maxims urging moderation in all things.

3. Delphi was believed to be the center of the earth's surface; an omphalos (perhaps a meteor fragment), representing the navel, was kept at the temple.

> **NOTE:** According to the mythologist Mircea Eliade, the phenomenon of pronouncing a place the center of the world is widespread in world religions. Not only does it generally signify the center of the world of humans, but it marks an axis going straight through the earth to heaven above and the Underworld below. Through this axis communication with the powers can take place. Interestingly, a culture may have several "centers"; it is thus often of more symbolic than geographic significance. Typical world axis places are temples and churches, large trees or posts erected in or outside the village, and mountaintops. The Maypole is probably a remnant of such a tradition.

4. Delphi was a holy site before Apollo's arrival there. According to tradition, there was a cleft in the rocks from which intoxicating vapors rose, but modern archaeologists have not been able to verify this.

5. The legend may be based on the idea that Delphic inspiration (breathing in) came from an earth goddess.

6. Aeschylus mentions the prehistory of Delphi: after Gaea came Themis, her daughter and Zeus's second wife, who taught Apollo the art of prophecy.

7. The origin of the Apollo worship at Delphi lies in the Olympic battle between male and female powers; according to the *Hymn to Pythian Apollo* Hera, to spite Zeus, gives birth to the serpent Typhon (Typhoeus) parthenogenically, entrusting his upbringing to the female dragon Python guarding the ancient sanctuary at Delphi.

8. Birth stories of heroes usually involve dangers for the child. Hera tries to prevent Leto from giving birth to Apollo and Artemis by not allowing her a safe place for her delivery and by not allowing the goddess of childbirth, Eileithyia, to assist. Athene persuades Hera to reconsider, and Apollo and Artemis are born on a floating island, transformed by Apollo into Delos.

9. The tale functions etiologically as an explanation of the name of Delos (brilliant), referring to the birth of the sun god.

10. Only three days old, Apollo shoots an arrow through the dragon Python, who has been ravaging the countryside. In his honor the virgin prophetess at the Oracle is called Pythia. The Pythian Games were celebrated every three years to commemorate the event.

NOTE: Apollo's slaying of the monster Python reflects the mythological pattern mentioned in chapter 6: the hero slaying the serpent or monster is a patriarchal perversion of an older theme. The serpent, which used to be one of the sacred symbols of the Great Goddess, has, within the patriarchal rule, become a monster that must be slain or tamed. Another common theme is incorporated in the story: the hero slaying monsters at a very early age. A similar story exists in American folklore, which claims (erroneously) that Davy Crockett killed a bear when he was three years old.

---

11. Acknowledging guilt at having killed the guardian of Gaea's shrine, Apollo exiles himself from Olympus to work as a shepherd. Hereby he creates a paradigm of expiation for mortals who seek to cleanse themselves of wrong-doing.

12. After his purification he returns to Delphi and inaugurates the first Pythia, who foretells the Trojan War.

13. Delphi represents a new order where guilt can be atoned rather than paid for in blood.

14. Every eight years the slaying of Python was reenacted in a religious drama, the *Stepterion,* by priests at Delphi.

15. The procedures at Delphi required ritual cleansing both of the customers and of the Pythia. An animal without imperfections was sacrificed, and the priestess entered an underground chamber where she, seated upon a tripod, inhaled sacred vapors from underground, drank sacred water, and chewed bay or laurel leaves. Then, in a trance, she uttered unintelligible words which a priest took down and translated into Greek verse.

16. The oracles are typically ambiguous. Many oracles have been preserved, such as the one advising King Croesus, planning to go to war with the Persians, that a great nation would fall if he crossed the Persian border.

17. During the two Persian invasions of Greece (490 and 480–479 B.C.), the oracle advised surrender in the beginning, but ended up supporting the defense of Greece with a "wooden wall," interpreted by the leader Themistocles to mean warships. Employing the fleet, the Greeks sank most of the Persian armada at the Battle of Salamis.

18. Sophocles uses the myth of Oedipus to confirm that no one can escape fulfilling Delphi's prophecies.

19. Delphi's prestige declined after the fifth century B.C. with first the demise of the city-state under Alexander the Great and later the Roman occupation of Greece.

20. Apollo was, despite his beauty, unlucky in love: the mountain nymph Daphne asked Zeus to transform her into a bay or laurel tree to escape Apollo's pursuit.

21. The youth Cyparissus loved his pet stag so much that when he accidentally kills it, he wants to die and ignores Apollo's pleas to transfer his affection to the god. Drained by weeping, Cyparissus is transformed into a cyprus.

22. The handsome boy Hyacinthus returns Apollo's affection but is fatally hit in the head by Apollo's hurtling discus. Apollo transforms the boy's body into a hyacinth flower.

23. Coronis, a princess of Thessaly, is already carrying Apollo's child when she falls in love with a mortal man. Apollo sends Artemis to kill Coronis, but the unborn child is preserved and given to Chiron, a centaur, to raise. The child, Asclepius, becomes the first physician.

24. When Asclepius learns to revive the dead, Zeus kills him with a thunderbolt; Apollo retaliates by killing the Cyclops who forged Zeus's lightning.

25. The cult of Asclepius was centered in Epidaurus and involved rituals with reptilian symbols, such as the caduceus interpreted sometimes as a phallic symbol but also as the Tree of Life, a Goddess symbol.

26. Using sympathetic magic, the Epidaurus physicians used the ancient Delphic rite of cleansing on their individual human patients.

> **PRIMARY TEXT SELECTION:** *Hymn to Pythian Apollo*

KEY NAMES OF MYTHOLOGICAL CHARACTERS MENTIONED

Apollo

Pythia, the priestess at the Oracle at Delphi

Themis, the goddess of eternal law, Gaea's daughter

Typhon (Typhoeus), the serpent son of Hera (Hesiod: Gaea's son)

Python, the female dragon guardian of Gaea's sanctuary at Delphi, the foster mother of Typhon

Themistocles, Athen's leader during the Persian wars

Daphne, a mountain nymph transformed into a bay or laurel tree

Cyparissus, a young man transformed into a cyprus

Hyacinthus, Apollo's lover killed by his discus and transformed into a flower

Coronis, the mother of Asclepius

Chiron, the wisest of Centaurs

Asclepius, son of Coronis and Apollo, the first physician

KEY NAMES ASSOCIATED WITH THE TELLING/CRITICISM OF MYTHS

Aeschylus (c. 525–456 B.C.)

Sophocles (c. 495–406 B.C.)

CHAPTER 8

DIONYSUS: ROOTED IN EARTH AND ECSTASY

MAIN POINTS

1.   Each winter Apollo left Delphi to live with the Hyperboreans, a mythical tribe in the North, and Dionysus moved into Delphi for those three months.

2.   The contrast between Apollo and Dionysus: moderation and mental balance versus an irrational power that allows people to explore their potential for emotional and behavioral extremes.

3.   Qualities in common: both sons of Zeus, they share his will to power and his creative drive; both are born under difficult circumstances; both establish cults; and both are associated with ecstasy, Apollo through the character of Pythia speaking in tongues (glossolalia) and Dionysus through the rapture of his followers.

4.   One theory is that Apollo and Dionysus are two sides of the same divinity, combining moderation and excess. This would make Apollo and Dionysus two equally important aspects of the human psyche.

5.   They both inspire poetry, song, and dance—Apollo with his lyre and Dionysus with his timbrel.

6.   Dionysus is commonly identified with other male fertility gods of the ancient Near East: Tammutz (Dumuzi), Adonis, and Osiris. They all share the same theme; they undergo a violent death, descend into the Underworld, and are reborn as immortal beings.

7.   Dionysus's entrance into Greece (either from Mycenae, Thrace, or Asia Minor) is presented in myth as ambiguous: he is both native born and brings a foreign cult to Greece.

8.   Euripides's play the *Bacchants* tells of Dionysus's (Bacchus's) return to Thebes from Asia Minor with a throng of Asian maenads.

9.   Dionysus's birth: Hera attempts to prevent Semele from giving birth to him; in disguise, she convinces Semele that her lover who visits her in the dark is an ogre. Semele persuades her lover to show himself as he really is, and when Zeus appears in a blaze of light, she is incinerated. From her corpse Zeus takes the embryo of Dionysus and places it in his thigh, from which Dionysus is born. (See Note, p. 31.)

10.   Springing from Zeus's genital area, Dionysus is a fertility god representing the growth, death, and rebirth of vegetation. He is a masculine counterpart of Persephone.

11.   The duality of Dionysus: His wine can induce mental disorientation as well as give pleasure; Dionysus himself, as a god of fluids, changes from a seductive adolescent to a savage bull.

30

NOTE: The story of the mortal woman or man who perishes by seeing the divine being in his or her true splendor is common. In Greek myth, it is found in stories such as Achteon perishing after seeing Artemis and Tiresias losing his sight after spying on Athene. In the Judeo-Christian tradition, Moses witnesses the presence of Yahweh in the shape of a burning bush, because the full view of God would kill him. A frequent theme in folklore mirrors the lovers' aspect of the story of Semele and Zeus. In the Norwegian fairytale of "East of the Sun and West of the Moon," the young woman's lover is a bewitched polar bear by day and a handsome prince by night; by sneaking a peak at his true nocturnal nature she ruins his chance of breaking the spell and becoming human again. However, since it is a fairytale, it does have a happy ending. A reversal of the theme happens in "Beauty and the Beast" and its variations where the young woman is *supposed* to "look beyond" the terrible facade to see her lover's true nature.

12. Two consistent themes in the myths of Dionysus are that he represents foreign customs and he confronts opponents hostile to him and his religion.

13. Hera continues her persecution of Dionysus; he is taken by Hermes to Semele's sister Ino who disguises him as a girl, but Hera drives Ino and her husband mad; Zeus now takes Dionysus abroad to Nysa and changes him into a young goat.

14. Dionysus's first lover, Ampelus, is gored to death by a bull, and Dionysus weeps for him; watered by his tears, Ampelus's body shoots forth a vine with grape clusters.

15. Dionysus teaches wine making to the gardener Icarius, who then travels around the countryside instructing farmers in viniculture. While dressed in the skin of a goat, he is murdered by shepherds.

16. Hera affects Dionysus with insanity (or drunkenness), compelling him to wander the earth. After his return to sanity he continues to travel. In Phrygia he is initiated into the orgiastic rites of Cybele. In Thrace he is imprisoned by King Lycurgus, and as punishment he strikes the country with sterility and the king with madness; then he has four horses tear the king's body to shreds.

17. When kidnaped by pirates, Dionysus changes them into dolphins, an etiological explanation of why dolphins are friendly to humans.

18. Dionysus acquires a retinue in India consisting of satyrs, which combine human shape and goat shape; the goat is the favored sacrificial animal in the Dionysian cult and the shape in which Dionysus himself appears.

19. Satyrs (Roman: fauns) are famous for their sexual prowess and are often depicted with exaggeratedly large and erect penises.

20. The selenius (a human with a horse's tail and hoofs), Bacchants (women followers), and Priapus (a fertility deity) follow Dionysus. Dionysus's worshipers carry the thyrsus, a staff topped with a pinecone and entwined with ivy.

21. In the sixth century B.C., an association was made between the myth of Dionysus and that of Orpheus. Both Dionysus and Orpheus experience a descent into Hades, a violent death, and deification. Orpheus also shares the bisexuality that characterizes Dionysus.

NOTE: Students may not be familiar with the tragedy of Orpheus and Eurydice at this point (see chapter 9). Eurydice, Orpheus's beloved wife, died from a snake bite, and Orpheus vowed to go to the Underworld to fetch her back. With his music he moved everyone in the Underworld, including Hades and Persephone, to such an extent that they allowed him to make an attempt to bring Eurydice with him to the land of the living, while playing his music. However, if he turned to look at her before they had safely arrived, she would be lost to him forever. Accompanied by Hermes, Eurydice's shadow began following her husband, but he moved quickly in anticipation of her rescue, and she could not keep up. When he arrived at the land of the living, he turned around to see her, but she was still enveloped by darkness; at that moment, Hermes whisked her back to the Underworld. In desperation, Orpheus tried a second time, but Charon wouldn't ferry him across to the Land of the Dead.

---

22. After the loss of Eurydice, Orpheus renounces women and captivates young men with his music. Some female Dionysus-followers tear him limb from limb in anger over being rejected and cast his body parts over the earth.

23. Some scholars believe that Orpheus's physical dismemberment suggests that, during prehistoric times, a young male was ritually sacrificed by being cut to pieces, which were then planted in the ground. There is not much evidence for this theory.

24. Orpheus was considered a source of occult knowledge because of his journey to Hades. The mystery cult Orphism offered spiritual guidance by expiating guilt and helping prepare the soul for its life after death. Orphism includes the idea of reincarnation, and the realm of Hades becomes a place of regeneration and rebirth.

25. Orphism promoted another variation of the Dionysian myth: Dionysus is the son of Zeus and Persephone; Zeus plans to enthrone his son as king of the universe; Hera induces the Titans to kill Dionysus by sparagmos. Athene saves the boy's heart, which she gives to Zeus, who swallows it and then impregnates Semele. Dionysus is reborn to Semele as Dionysus Zagreus.

26. Zeus kills the Titans with his thunderbolt; humans spring from the ashes of the Titans and are thus descendants of rebel Titans as well as the divine flesh of Dionysus, so humans carry a divine spark within them.

27. Orphism taught that the body is a prison (soma sema), and death frees the soul.

28. The festival for Dionysus, the Dionysia, featured a procession with followers carrying a statue of the god and replicas of his phallus. The Dionysian Mysteries were very popular in Greece and Italy and persisted well into the Christian era.

29. Orphism created a balance between the passion of Dionysus and the austerity of Apollo, suggesting a unity of the two gods. Orphism anticipated many doctrines of Christianity, and early Christians used the figure of Orpheus or Dionysus to depict Jesus.

PRIMARY TEXT SELECTION: *Hymn to Dionysus*

KEY NAMES OF MYTHOLOGICAL CHARACTERS MENTIONED

Apollo

Dionysus

Bacchus, another name for Dionysus

Semele, Dionysus's mother

Hera

Ino, Semele's sister

Ampelus, Dionysus's first lover, the origin of winegrapes

Icarius, the first viniculturist

Satyrs, half-human and half-goat, part of Dionysus's entourage

Selenius, a humanoid creature with horse tail and hooves

Bacchants, female followers of Dionysus

Priapus, a fertility god depicted with an erection

Orpheus, Eurydice's husband, musician, bisexual

Titans, offspring of Gaea, killed by Zeus

KEY NAMES ASSOCIATED WITH THE TELLING/CRITICISM OF MYTHS

Euripides (c. 485–406 B.C.)

CHAPTER 9

LAND OF NO RETURN:
THE GLOOMY KINGDOM OF HADES

MAIN POINTS

1. While the gods represent the Greek desire for perpetual youth, beauty, and eternal life, myths about the heroes show awareness of the finality of life and of every valued quality.

2. In the *Odyssey,* Homer shows the Greek dread of Hades: when Odysseus learns that he must descend into Hades's realm, he feels terror, since death represents perpetual imprisonment in the dark. Odysseus faces both his own mortality and the fate of the soul after death.

3. In the Underworld, Achilles tells Odysseus that he would rather be a poor man's living slave than king of the dead.

4. The Homeric view of Hades is the oldest and most influential view of the afterlife in Greek tradition. It shows the finality of life as well as the impossibility of contact between the living and the dead.

5. The souls in Hades have lost memory, reason, and willpower.

6. Odysseus performs a ritual to summon the dead and communicate with them by digging a trench for them to drink from; the trench symbolizes both the grave and the boundary between life and death. The drink consists of elements of the earth's bounty as well as blood.

7. Odysseus travels westward to Hades across the River of Ocean, the earth's boundary. His journey parallels that of Gilgamesh traveling to the retreat of Utnapishtim.

8. The Homeric concept of the afterlife resembles Mesopotamian beliefs about the Underworld. According to the Hebrew Bible, the dead, good and bad, are kept in an underground region, Sheol, where there is nothing but inactivity.

9. Five rivers were said to flow through the Underworld: the Styx, the Acheron, Cocytus, Phlegethon, and a "river of unmindfulness" that runs through the plain of Lethe. The Romans called the river Lethe and made it the waters of forgetfulness to be drunk by souls before being reincarnated.

10. In the Homeric paradise of Elysium or the Isles of the Blest, a few heroes are allowed to spend the afterlife, such as Helen's husband, Menelaus.

11. Hades represents death, and Persephone, otherwise associated with youth and flowers, takes on the same quality of pitilessness; only a few dead are allowed to return to earth, and they generally accentuate the inevitability of loss.

12. Hades is also the place for monsters such as the multiheaded hound of hell called Cerberus, the Furies, and the Gorgons.

13. Mythographers after Homer had the souls cross the river by boat to arrive in Hades. The ferryman, Charon, demanded money for his services, so it was a Greek custom to bury the dead with coins in their hands or mouth.

14. Two judges reside in Hades, Minos and his brother Rhadamanthus; Plato adds a third judge, Aeacus. In later traditions, these judges would determine the fate of the dead souls.

15. Thanatos (Death) has a brother, Hypnos (Sleep); Hypnos's son Morpheus, the god of dreams, shows himself to sleepers in human shape, sometimes bringing messages from the dead.

16. Hesiod introduces Tartarus as an elemental deity as well as an amorphous abyss into which the Titans are thrown. Tartarus foreshadows the Christian notion of hell.

17. Homer tells of three criminals suffering in Hades: Tityus tried to rape Leto and is punished by being spread-eagled and having two vultures feed on his liver.

18. Tantalus stands in a pool of water but is unable to slake his thirst, because the water recedes when he bends over; he can't reach grapes growing overhead for the same reason. There are several different accounts of his crime: he stole the ambrosia of the gods and gave it to humans; he told secrets from the table of the gods; and he served the flesh of his son to the gods.

19. Sisyphus is forced to roll a boulder uphill, only to have it roll back again, so that he must endlessly repeat that meaningless task. Sisyphus is being punished for tricking the gods into letting him go back to earth from Hades once, and hiding out until he died of old age.

NOTE: The character of Sisyphus became an important symbol for the existential philosophical movement of the mid-twentieth century: The French novelist Albert Camus sees him as a symbol of a human being, realizing that life is, in essence, absurd, since there are no pre-established, god-given rules. Each task is as meaningless as rolling the boulder uphill and watching it roll down again. Camus's twist to the story is to suggest that Sisyphus takes control of his life and obtains freedom from the slavery of absurdity by *choosing* to perform these meaningless tasks. See chapter 23; see also "Note" on Odysseus's father in chapter 12 on page 51.

---

20. Ixion assaulted Hera and is in Hades bound to a perpetually rolling fiery wheel.

21. Later myths view Tartarus as the place where all human souls go to be purged and punished.

22. In Greco-Roman myth, only a few heroes travel to the netherworld (katabasis) and come back alive, usually as part of a trial or personal development.

23. Symbolically the hero endures death and rebirth, and renews his purpose in life, such as Odysseus and Aeneas do.

24. The hero's successful descent is usually sponsored by an Olympian protector, such as Athene supporting Odysseus and Heracles, Aphrodite supporting Aeneas, and love (Eros), which motivates Orpheus and Dionysus.

25. Heracles, initiated into the Mysteries of Demeter and sponsored by Athene and Hermes, travels to the Underworld as the last of his Twelve Labors to kidnap the hound Cerberus. With Hades's (Pluto's) permission he captures the dog with his bare hands; in addition he liberates Asclepius and gets Theseus released.

26. Heracles can return to the gods in spirit, but his image must remain in Hades. Homer here anticipates the later theory of the dual nature of immortal mind and mortal body.

27. Orpheus travels to Hades to rescue his beloved wife, Eurydice, dead from a snake bite. With his music he moves Hades and Persephone to tears, and they let him take her with him, provided that he promises not to look at her during the ascent. However, he can't help himself; when he turns around to see her, he loses her to Hades forever.

28. According to early Christian writers, Jesus entered the netherworld on Good Friday to retrieve righteous souls who died before he had opened the way to heaven: "the harrowing of hell" in medieval theology.

29. Even in the Homeric Underworld the soul retains some of its individuality. The Homeric view of Hades is like a Freudian or Jungian dreamlike state of paralysis.

30. Greek philosophers came to believe that moral absolutes exist and that souls will be dealt with after death according to whether they were good or evil in life. Pythagoras, Plato, and others envisioned a compartmentalized Hades.

NOTE: Pythagoras reportedly believed in reincarnation, and there is some evidence (in the dialogues *Phaedo* and *Phaedrus*) that Plato may have agreed. In *Phaedrus,* Plato lets Socrates describe the cycle of life and death as a movement of the soul between the world of matter and the world of spirit. While in the world of spirit, the soul is all-knowing and shares the company of the Forms, the eternal ideas that give meaning and reality to life on earth. Then, because of an imperfect previous life, the soul is compelled to be reborn into the world of matter, the world we know as reality, which for Plato is a shadowland of imperfection. However, the more we realize that the world of the Forms is the true reality (in other words, the more we become true philosophers), the closer we are to not having to be reborn again. See also chapter 19.

---

31. The notion of the Underworld has a dual nature: the place for the psyche's destructive potential and a projection of the hope for immortality.

32. In the *Aeneid,* Virgil portrays Aeneas's descent into the land of the dead as an exploration of the human subconscious, and he realizes that the Underworld is both the tomb and the womb of life.

KEY NAMES OF MYTHOLOGICAL CHARACTERS MENTIONED

Odysseus, the Homeric hero of Troy and the eponymous hero of the Odyssey

Achilles, the hero of the *Iliad*

Thanatos, the personification of death

Circe, a sorceress in the *Odyssey*

Gilgamesh, the king of Uruk

Enkidu, his friend

Sheol, the Hebrew Underworld

Styx, Acheron, Cocytus, Phlegethon: rivers in Hades

Lethe, a plain in Hades; Roman: the river of forgetfulness

Elysium, a paradise for select heroes

Menelaus, the husband of Helen of Troy

Aidoneus, another name for Hades (Pluto)

Persephone

Orpheus, a musician, the inspiration for Orphism

Cerberus, the hound of hell

Charon, the ferryman of Hades

Minos, Rhadamanthus, the Aeacus, judges in Hades

Hypnos, the god of sleep

Morpheus, the god of dreams

Tartarus

Tityus, a sinner in Tartarus/Hades, punished by vultures feeding on his liver

Tantalus, a sinner in Tartarus/Hades, punished by eternal hunger and thirst

Sisyphus, a sinner in Tartarus/Hades, punished by repeatedly rolling a rock uphill

Ixion, a sinner in Tartarus/Hades, punished by being bound to a rolling wheel of fire

Heracles, the strong demi-god

Athene

Hermes

Psychopompos, Hermes's name as a guide of the soul

KEY NAMES ASSOCIATED WITH THE TELLING/CRITICISM OF MYTHS

Homer (ninth century B.C.)

Anacreon, Greek lyric poet (sixth century B.C.)

Pythagoras, Greek philosopher and mathematician (sixth century B.C.)

Plato, Greek philosopher (c. 427–347 B.C.)

Virgil, Roman poet (70–19 B.C.)

CHAPTER 10

THE HERO: MAN DIVIDED AGAINST HIMSELF

MAIN POINTS

1. Perseus, one of the earliest Greek heroes, shares some characteristics with later heroes, but an important difference is that he maintains mutually supportive relationships with women.

2. Perseus's mother, Danae, was visited in her bronze tower prison by Zeus, appearing as a shower of gold. By imprisoning her, her father, Acrisius, was trying to prevent the fulfilling of a prophecy that a son of Danae would kill him.

3. At Perseus's birth, Acrisius puts him and Danae to sea in a chest (symbol of coffin and womb). They land safely on the island of Seriphus where Perseus is raised by the fisherman Dictys.

4. Dictys's brother, King Polydectes, desires Danae, who rejects him. Perseus offers to bring him a gift instead, and the king asks for the head of Medusa.

5. Perseus receives help from Athene telling him to visit the Graeae, three old hags with one eye and one tooth between them. Snatching the eye, Perseus forces them to help him find magical weapons: a pouch, a pair of winged sandals, and a cape of invisibility. In addition, Perseus has a polished bronze shield.

6. The Graeae and the Gorgon represent the deadly aspect of the Great Goddess, tamed by Perseus, an inversion of the castration of Uranus.

7. In Freudian theory, decapitation is an unconscious image of castration.

8. This does not imply that Perseus rejects the feminine powers; his weapons are less aggressive than those of typical heroes.

9. At the Gorgon's cave, Perseus finds petrified statues of men who have looked at the face of Medusa. With his cape of invisibility, Perseus safely sees Medusa's reflection in his shield and cuts off her head; the winged horse Pegasus springs from her neck.

10. In Ethiopia, Perseus saves the princess Andromeda from being sacrificed to a sea monster; he kills the monster by showing it the head of Medusa, which he has kept in the magic pouch.

11. Perseus returns home, completing the heroic rite of passage: departure, testing, triumph, and return.

12. He saves his mother from Polydectes by showing him Medusa's head; afterwards he returns his weapons to Hermes and gives the head of the Gorgon to Athene, who places it on her shield.

13. Perseus may represent a shift in the hero image from a matriarchal to a patriarchal system; his quest involves aiding women and receiving help from women. In addition, his quest ends happily with marriage to Andromeda.

14. Following his return, Perseus accidentally kills his grandfather with a discus throw, fulfilling the prophecy. Reluctant to take over his grandfather's throne, Perseus trades cities with his cousin and becomes the ruler of Tiryns and Mycenae.

15. An early function of the Perseus myth is etiological, explaining the origin of several constellations.

16. Thus, Perseus succeeds in achieving immortality in the heavens.

17. A new patriarchal type of hero succeeds Perseus: Bellerophon riding the Pegasus.

18. Heracles is also half-human, half-divine, being the son of Zeus and Alcmene, but he is not as harmonious a man as Perseus.

19. Heracles's characteristics: unnaturally brave and strong, protective of society, and capable of animal-like behavior.

20. Heracles embodies the heroic predicament of how to fulfill the demand for godlike knowledge and achievement while bound to a mortal body. At the same time, such a hero is a threat to the gods.

21. The hero figure is isolated by his own uniqueness in striving toward excess and immortality. Gilgamesh also personifies this trait.

22. This isolation extends to relationships with women, since domestic contentment is considered destructive to the heroic task.

23. Hera attempts to kill Heracles by sending a serpent into his cradle.

24. Heracles's nature involves extremes of animal brutality and sexual appetite as well as social services. He embodies the question of how a hero settles down after leaving the battlefield.

25. The Twelve Labors include: killing the Nemean lion, killing the Hydra, capturing the Cerynitian hind, capturing the Erymanthian boar, cleaning the Augean stables, removing the Stymphalian birds, capturing the Cretan bull, capturing the Thracian horses, bringing back the girdle of Hippolyte, bringing back the cattle of Geryon, bringing back the Golden Apples of the Hesperides, and capturing Cerberus.

26. The Twelve Labors are Heracles's punishment for killing his wife, Megara, and their children in a fit of rage.

27. Heracles fulfills the hero's most significant function: to extend the parameters of human experience, imagination, and knowledge.

28. In his journeys to the Underworld, he transcends the limits of the human condition and achieves a form of immortality.

29. A mythic anachronism exists in Heracles's voyage with Jason and the Argonauts, since the story of Jason takes place several generations after Heracles.

30. Heracles's death is caused by his new wife, Deianeira, who, searching for her husband, is raped by the centaur Nessus. Wounded by Heracles, Nessus tells Deianeira that she can make her husband faithful to her by smearing his blood and semen on his shirt; the mixture eats through the shirt and his flesh and kills him.

31. Some versions of the myth explain that Heracles's soul goes to the Underworld, while his reputation is immortal. Other versions tell of his upraising to heaven by the gods. Homer says that his human part remains in Hades while his divine self resides with the gods.

32. Characteristics shared by other heroes: divine ancestry, performing amazing feats or pursuing impossible quests, having a problem with women, and suffering nonheroic deaths.

33. Theseus's absent father Aegeus leaves a sword and a pair of sandals under a stone for his son to find and claim his political inheritance.

34. There are similarities between Theseus and Heracles, such as Theseus carrying a club, killing a wild boar, and capturing the same Cretan bull; in addition, Theseus joins Heracles on two expeditions, and Heracles rescues Theseus from the Underworld.

35. Theseus's most famous exploit is his adventure on Crete. Volunteering to go as one of the fourteen Athenians to be devoured by the Minotaur in order to put an end to the threat, Theseus, with the help of Ariadne and Daedalus, kills the Minotaur and escapes from the labyrinth by following Ariadne's unrolled ball of string.

36. Upon his return to Athens, Theseus forgets to substitute the white sail for the black sail (the prearranged message to his father that he had survived). Grieving over his son's supposed death, the father throws himself off the cliff.

37. Theseus's relationships with women are unhappy, like those of Heracles. He abandons Ariadne on the island of Naxos on the way home; he seduces/defeats the Amazon Queen Hippolyte, and their son Hippolytus is falsely accused of rape by Theseus's wife, Phaedra, and put to death.

38. Theseus is trapped in the Underworld after a scheme to kidnap Persephone for his friend Pirithous; both men are bound in Hades, but Heracles saves Theseus.

39. Despite political problems Theseus unifies Athens.

40. Some scholars see the myth of the Minotaur as a political shift in power at the end of the Minoan era.

41. Theseus dies by either falling or being pushed from a cliff, repeating the death of his father. He is immortalized as a god afterwards.

42. Jason is the son of Aeson of Iolcos and the grandson of Aeolus, the wind god. Aeson's brother, Pelias, usurped the throne of Iolcos. When Jason is born, his parents have him raised in secret by the centaur Chiron.

43. When the adult Jason returns to Iolcos wearing only one sandal, Pelias believes him to be his prophesied killer, so Pelias gives Jason an impossible mission to get rid of him.

44. The mission is to fetch the Golden Fleece in Colchis. Jason organizes an expedition of Argonauts (sailors on the ship *Argos*).

45. Hera wants Pelias dead, and to this end she wants Jason to bring Medea back from Colchis with him. Medea helps Jason retrieve the fleece.

46. As a condition for giving Jason the fleece, the king of Colchis demands that he sow a field with dragon's teeth and fight the armed men who germinate from the teeth. With Medea's help he succeeds, but the king refuses to part with the fleece.

47. Medea puts the fleece-guarding dragon to sleep with magic, and Jason steals the fleece; to prevent pursuit by her father, Medea kills and dismembers her younger brother, tossing the pieces into the sea so that her father will be delayed by funeral rituals.

48. The power of Hecate helps Jason obtain the fleece and escape; Jason's quest is less heroic than quests of previous heroes since it deteriorates into a search for wealth and status.

49. On their return Medea tricks Pelias's daughters by persuading them that Pelias will be rejuvenated if they kill him, dismember him, and cook him. The people of Iolcos refuse to accept Jason as their new ruler, and he and Medea must leave.

50. After emigrating to Corinth, Jason leaves Medea and their two children to marry the princess of Corinth, and Medea poisons the princess and her father, King Creon, and kills her own children. She then flees to the realm of King Aegeus to restore his fertility; the child he fathers is Theseus.

51. Jason dies when a ship's beam hits him on the head; contrary to previous heroes, he is not elevated to divine status.

52. Heracleian hero myths often emphasize that the hero is half-human and half-divine; other myths give an alternative perspective by reminding the Greeks of the ideal of moderation.

53. Icarus, son of Daedalus, is given a pair of wax wings by his father so that they can escape the wrath of King Minos, after Daedalus helped Theseus. Icarus does not heed his father's advice of moderate flying, and flies so close to the sun that his wings melt; he falls into the sea and drowns.

NOTE: The ideal of moderation became an integral part of later Greek virtue ethics. In the fourth century B.C., the philosopher Aristotle outlined the rule of the Golden Mean, which states that a good person must strive for the proper balance between too much and too little effort and feeling. The flight of Icarus is traditionally used as an example of *hubris,* overblown confidence in oneself, but since Icarus refuses to listen to his father's advice of not flying too low or too high, it is also a classic example of the Greek moral value of doing things in the right amount, not too much or too little. See also chapter 23.

54. Phaethon, the son of Helios, asks his father if he can drive the chariot of the sun for a day. Helios agrees, but Phaethon loses control of the horses, creating the Milky Way and setting fire to the earth. To save the earth, Zeus kills Phaethon with a lightning bolt. Moral: Being half-divine does not grant you divine powers.

55. Centaurs, half-human and half-horse, embody both brains and brawn. When invited to the wedding of a Lapith princess, they drink too much and attempt to rape and carry off the Lapith women.

56. In contrast Chiron is temperate and wise, instructing Asclepius in the art of medicine. He tries to stop the centaurs' rampage at the Lapith wedding, only to be shot by Heracles's arrow. He offers to take Prometheus's place, releasing him from the rock.

KEY NAMES OF MYTHOLOGICAL CHARACTERS MENTIONED

Perseus, Greek hero

Danae, his mother

Acrisius, her father

Dictys, Perseus's foster father

King Polydectes, Dictys's brother

Athene

The Graeae, three old hags with one eye between them

Medusa, one of the three Gorgon sisters; turns men into stone

Pegasus, the winged horse

Andromeda, Ethiopian princess, later Perseus's wife

Hermes

Bellerophon, Pegasus's rider

Heracles, the strong hero

Gilgamesh, king of Uruk

Hera

Megara, Heracles's first wife

Jason, Greek hero, grandson of the wind god Aeolus

The Argonauts, Jason's fellow heroes, the crew of the ship *Argos*

Deianeira, Heracles's second wife

Nessus, a centaur

Theseus, Greek hero, son of Aethra and Aegeus (or Poseidon)

Aegeus, his father, the king of Athens

Ariadne, daughter of King Minos

Daedalus, Minoan inventor

Hippolyte, the Amazon queen

Hippolytus, her son with Theseus, accused of raping Phaedra

Phaedra, Ariadne's sister, Theseus's wife

Jason, Greek hero

Aeson of Iolcos, his father

Pelias, Aeson's brother

Chiron, the centaur who reared Jason and taught Asclepius

Medea, the daughter of Aeetes, king of Colchis

Daedalus, Minoan inventor, the designer of the Labyrinth

Icarus, his son

Phaethon, son of Helios and mortal Clymene

Helios, the sun god

Asclepius, the first physician

Prometheus, the Titan who stole fire from the gods

CHAPTER 11

HEROES AT WAR: THE TROY SAGA

MAIN POINTS

1. The decision of Paris is important because it is a paradigm of the complex world of myth and because it is the source of inspiration for many other myths.

2. Zeus has arranged a wedding between Thetis, a minor sea goddess, and a mortal man, Peleus; all the gods are invited except Eris, the goddess of strife, who shows up anyway with a golden apple "for the fairest."

NOTE: The theme of the goddess who is not invited and who shows up with a curse is a familiar folklore motif: Sleeping Beauty (Grimm: Little Briar Rose) sleeps because the thirteenth Wise Woman who was *not* invited to a feast in Beauty's honor (twelve were invited, because the king has twelve gold plates) cursed her with death, a curse ameliorated by the other women. In folklore, goddesses or fates often punish people with curses for their neglect.

---

3. Hera, Athene, and Aphrodite quarrel over the golden apple, so Zeus throws it off Mount Olympus. It lands in a field outside of Troy, where King Priam's son Paris is tending sheep.

4. The goddesses offer him gifts in exchange for the golden apple: Hera offers power over Asia Minor, Athene offers wisdom, and Aphrodite offers the love of the most beautiful woman in the world. Paris gives the apple to Aphrodite.

5. Priam sends Paris on a diplomatic mission to Sparta; he meets Helen, wife of King Menelaus, daughter of a mortal woman, Leda, and Zeus, who visited Leda in the shape of a swan.

6. While Paris is a guest in their home, Menelaus leaves on a trip, and Paris seduces or abducts Helen. When Paris refuses to return her, Priam feels honor-bound to defend him; Menelaus has allies who come to his support, and the Trojan War begins.

7. The implications of the story of the judgment of Paris involve sequels, because Greek myth is essentially open-ended.

8. Myths occur in a timeless or nonchronological world. Thus, Achilles, son of Thetis and Peleus, would be too young to take part in the battle of Troy, but he is a renowned hero at its beginning. Human time cannot be meaningfully applied to mythic time.

9. Zeus sanctifies family values and social order; Paris violates this order, but family loyalty is also a value under the old clan and kinship system, and Priam's adherence to this value makes the value systems clash.

10. The cosmos itself is not stable; change is in the nature of things, and the gods must cope with the existence of evil. The disharmony in the human world reflects that of the cosmos.

11. The human and the divine are closely connected: humans and gods can intermarry, but they rarely understand each other. Thetis tries to immortalize her son Achilles by dipping him in the divine fire, holding him by the heel. This heel remains his mortal, parental heritage: the "Achilles's heel" *is* the human condition.

12. The gods lack power over human fate; humans have, in a limited sense, freedom to act but must bear the responsibility of their actions. By making a choice, Paris defines himself, as the other heroes do, and each lives the life and death he has chosen.

13. The *Iliad* and the *Odyssey* are attributed to Homer, who may have lived on an island off the coast of Asia Minor between 800 and 700 B.C. Legend depicts him as blind, but it may be a traditional attribute of a prophet who sees moral truths, undistracted by surface appearances.

14. Both poems have signs of oral composition, such as fixed epithets and adjectives, and they share quality of style; however, their perspectives on certain issues differ radically.

15. The poet may have changed his mind, later editors may have made changes, or the poems may have been composed by different poets but recorded by the same editor.

16. Both poems use inherited mythic material, adding the device of dialogue and omniscient narrator, shaping the material into the form of the epic containing formal conventions. These conventions include the proem, the semidivinity of the hero, and the hero's katabasis.

17. The choice of the epic form establishes the author's conviction of the seriousness of the story, and the epic is itself an expression of pride in one's civilization.

18. Contrary to the myth, the epic is rooted in human time. The poet continually reminds us about the passage of time.

19. Homer's epic poems are not open-ended like the myth, but have a narrative plot structure.

20. Homer uses epic similes to make the supernatural experiences understandable.

21. In addition, Homer uses cliff-hangers and flashbacks to shape the material. He interrupts the chase scene in the *Iliad* to describe the everyday experience of women doing laundry; this contrasts the situation of the heroes with the everyday values they are fighting to uphold.

22. The *Iliad*'s focus is the quarrel between Achilles and Agamemnon and its consequences. The purpose is to explore questions such as: What does it mean to be a hero? How can a hero create a meaningful life for himself in the face of certain death?

23. The heroes are divided beings: they must be warriors, because it is their nature, but this means that they must violate their needs as social beings.

24. Achilles has two possible fates: a long life in obscurity or a short, brilliant one in battle. For both Hector and Achilles to choose inaction means the death of the soul; however, the immortality of honor implies physical death.

25. The hero's reputation must be publicly confirmed by the community, and true heroism can be confused with the external signs of public approval.

26. Enraged by grief, Achilles believes that he can transcend human needs; only after Hector's death does he recognize the needs of the body and reconcile with Priam and the community. Similarly, Hector confuses honor with blind loyalty.

27. A moderate alternative is Diomedes, who has courage but not to excess. But it is not until the fifth century B.C. that the qualities exhibited by Diomedes would become the moral ideal.

28. Odysseus is the most intelligent of the Greek warriors—and the best speaker. He uses a disguise to spy on the Trojans and invents the ruse of the Trojan Horse, but his nature of using deception makes him an ambiguous hero.

29. The gods take sides: Hera, Poseidon, and Athene side with the Greeks, and Apollo, Artemis, and Aphrodite favor the Trojans. Zeus is neutral.

30. The gods intervene in human affairs, either as aggressors or as targets, but even when they are wounded, they do not die; the war is a game to them.

31. The gods of the *Iliad* are not omnipotent; they can't control fate or human behavior. They do reinforce values such as courtesy and the guest-host relationship. Since the Trojans have broken these rules, they must lose in the end.

32. The human connection to the gods happens through their gratitude toward the gods and through rituals. The gods do not necessarily reward the humans accordingly.

33. Human beings determine their own fate; the dual destinies show that fate is not predetermined but conditional.

34. Zeus uses scales to weigh the fate of humans, but he does not control them.

35. The two urns from which Zeus doles out gifts are the image of the human condition: it is not possible to have a life without at least some suffering.

36. The heroic code is ambivalent: we admire the dedication and courage of heroes, but we see how such attributes turn to excess. While the code calls for high ideals, it also encourages contempt for inferiors.

37. The ideal, the single combat, is not to defeat the enemy but to enhance one's reputation. However, it is ultimately a no-win situation.

38. The real victims are the women: some are used as war booty or prizes in games; even those who are not slaves are equally trapped in the social expectations. Helen herself is not loved by Menelaus; Agamemnon despises his wife. Of the Greeks, only Odysseus has a happy family life. The Greek family bonds are typically between father and son.

39. Hector and his wife, Andromache, are devoted to each other, and their household is a model family; ironically, the Greeks who represent family values have abandoned their own families to go to war, while the transgressors of family values, the Trojans, are depicted as ideal models of family love.

40. Andromache sees the truth that Hector's urge to fight is destructive to the family.

41. Hector and Achilles can't acknowledge their anima; the exclusively masculine heroic code is destructive to families and civilization, but it was part of Bronze Age ethics: making war was masculine, staying at home was feminine.

42. Homer comments ironically on the limits of the heroic model, and the women are given the last word in the *Iliad*. Even so, the focus is on the hero; the *Odyssey* changes the focus into a reconciliation of opposites of masculine and feminine.

43. The *Iliad* ends with Hector's funeral, on a conciliatory note.

44. The rite of passage for Achilles is not literal, but to a hell within and back. After undergoing separation and alienation, he is reconciled with the community.

45. The myth tells of the death of Achilles: he is killed by a shot to the heel by Paris or Apollo. The war goes on, involving additional tests for the Greeks through prophecies.

46. The war is not concluded until Odysseus thinks of creating the Trojan Horse as a peace offering. The horse, being hollow, contains Odysseus and his men, who emerge from the horse at night and open the gates of Troy. The men of Troy are killed, and women and children are taken prisoner.

KEY NAMES OF MYTHOLOGICAL CHARACTERS MENTIONED

Zeus

Thetis, a sea goddess, Achilles's mother

Peleus, Achilles's father

Eris, goddess of strife

Hera

Athene

Aphrodite

King Priam, ruler of Troy

Paris, his son

King Menelaus, king of Sparta

Helen, his wife, the most beautiful woman in the world

Leda, Helen's mother

Hector, Priam's son, Paris's brother

Diomedes, the moderate warrior

Andromache, Hector's wife

KEY NAMES ASSOCIATED WITH THE TELLING/CRITICISM OF MYTHS

Homer (ninth century B.C.)

CHAPTER 12

A DIFFERENT KIND OF HERO:
THE QUEST OF ODYSSEUS

MAIN POINTS

1. A popular Greek tradition assumes that the *Iliad* is a work from Homer's youth and that the *Odyssey* is a product of his old age. Some modern critics assume that the *Odyssey*'s author is a woman.

2. Constructional differences: The *Iliad* takes place in a limited space, whereas the *Odyssey*'s world is the entire Mediterranean basin, and a tour of heaven, earth, and Hades as well.

NOTE: The geography of the *Odyssey*, while traditionally well mapped, has recently acquired a new, highly controversial interpretation: The Italian nuclear physicist Felice Vinci has, based on his research of Plutarch, published the theory that Calypso's island Ogygie is not in the Mediterranean, but one of the Faroe Islands (Denmark), which indeed include an island named Hogoyggi. On the basis of this anchor point, Vinci remaps the travels of Odysseus to include the coast of Norway (Scheria), Zealand of Denmark (Pelops), and the island of Bornholm with the town Nexo (Naxos). Ithaca itself he pronounces to be the Danish island of Lyo. He locates Troy by the town of Toija in Finland, and explains the shift in geography to Greece and the Mediterranean by a deterioration of the Nordic climate around 1600 B.C. that prompted a mass exodus south by the members of the local Bronze Age culture who brought their tales of war with them. Vinci supports his claims by pointing out that the weather in the Homeric poems is always cold and foggy, and the Greeks are described as fair-haired. Most classicists remain skeptical of his interpretation, however.

---

3. The structure of the poem: Odysseus does not appear until book 5 of the *Odyssey*; the first four books describe conditions in Ithaca in his absence. The story itself covers the six weeks between Odysseus's departure from Calypso's island until his revenge on the suitors at Ithaca.

4. The central section tells of his exploits before arriving at Calypso's island. The end of the book focuses on his return to his home.

5. Odysseus is defined by his intelligence, making him an extraordinary epic hero who uses cunning rather than force. In addition, he has fully human parents (Laertes and Anticleia), in contrast to most Greek heroes, including Achilles.

NOTE: According to Sophocles and several other Greek sources, Odysseus's natural father was not Laertes, the old man anxiously awaiting his son's return, but the wily Sisyphus, who seduced Laertes's wife, Anticleia, during an argument with her father over stolen horses. This parentage was supposed to account for the cunning of Odysseus, since Sisyphus was the only human ever cunning enough to fool Hades into letting him go back to earth after death. For his cunning, Sisyphus was later punished in the Underworld.

6. Odysseus does not have the heroic stature of Achilles, either; he dons disguises, and Athene helps him look taller and handsomer when the situation requires it. This accentuates Odysseus's chameleon-like character.

7. Achilles argues for bravery, while Odysseus advocates prudence; the heroic warriors obsessed with personal glory die in battle, while Odysseus lives until old age.

8. The moral universe of the *Odyssey* reflects the idea of heavenly justice: people bring suffering on themselves, exceeding what evil Necessity brings.

9. Zeus's example: Aegisthus, who murdered Agamemnon and was slain by his son Orestes. The example illustrates three issues: (1) If the suitors kill Odysseus, his son must revenge him; (2) Odysseus will cause many of his own problems; and (3) there is retributive justice in the law of the Olympians.

10. Odysseus violates his own standards of prudence when (1) he loots the city of Ismarus and (2) during the encounter with Polyphemus when he speaks his true name.

11. For his act of blinding the Cyclops, Poseidon delays his homecoming for ten years, leading to his descent into the Underworld to ask Tiresias's advice and eventually to Odysseus's acceptance of the role of a nobody, deprived of identity as well as clothing.

12. Athene, the goddess of wisdom, is Odysseus's protector, and acting as his Mentor, restores order in Ithaca.

13. Post-Homeric traditions create sequels to the *Odyssey* such as the narrative poem *Telegonia.*

14. Circe and Calypso represent isolated cultural pockets where the Goddess still rules. Circe's feminine power threatens Odysseus's masculine identity, until Hermes helps him; once they are equals, they can establish a partnership.

15. As a representative of the Goddess, as well as of Odysseus's anima, Circe reveals the path to the Underworld, how to avoid Scylla and Charybdis, how to withstand the song of the Sirens, and how to refrain from eating the sacred cattle of Helios.

16. Calypso represents another threat, the demands of sexuality. The middle-aged Odysseus is under such nightly demands, while during the day he is deprived of challenges.

17. She offers to make Odysseus immortal, but he chooses to go home to his aging wife. The offer may echo the custom of sacrificing the consort of the Goddess, thus making him immortal in death.

18. Odysseus's refusal sets him apart from other heroes who seek immortality; he chooses to remain an earthly human and accept the natural law of the life cycle expressed by the Great Goddess.

19. He is reminiscent of early heroes such as Perseus and Heracles, but exceeds them in his solitariness.

20. In the Underworld, Agamemnon warns Odysseus not to trust any wife; Odysseus, however, has full trust in Penelope, who is his partner in intelligence and resourcefulness; this is evident in her delaying tactics with the suitors and in the ruse about moving the marriage bed.

21. Penelope functions as a priestess of the Goddess; she embodies her husband's anima, which is rejoined with her animus; in this she is the hero's counterpart.

22. The homecoming concludes the *Odyssey*, but the story implies further travels to placate Poseidon.

> **PRIMARY TEXT SELECTION:** Homer, *Odyssey*

KEY NAMES OF MYTHOLOGICAL CHARACTERS MENTIONED

Odysseus, Greek warrior of the siege of Troy

Laertes, his father

Anticleia, his mother

Athene

Achilles, the hero of the siege of Troy

Aegisthus, the lover of Clytemnestra, and killer of her husband, Agamemnon

Agamemnon, leader of the Greeks at Troy

Orestes, the son of Clytemnestra and Agamemnon

Telemachus, the son of Odysseus

Polyphemus, the Cyclops, son of Poseidon

Circe, a sorceress; Odysseus's lover for a year

Calypso, a nymph; Odysseus's lover for seven years

Tiresias, the blind seer in Hades

Penelope, Odysseus's wife

Poseidon

KEY NAMES ASSOCIATED WITH THE TELLING/CRITICISM OF MYTHS

Homer (ninth century B.C.)

Apollodorus (c. 140 B.C.)

Dante Alighieri, Italian poet (1265–1321)

Alfred, Lord Tennyson, English poet (1809–1892)

CHAPTER 13

THE THEATER OF DIONYSUS AND THE TRAGIC VISION

MAIN POINTS

1. The philosopher Friedrich Nietzsche argued that Greek art reached its creative peak in the Greek tragedy when the Apollonian sense of distinct identity and the Dionysian passion formed a synthesis.

2. The Great Dionysia, held annually for five days in March, included a procession of citizens carrying emblems of the Dionysus cult and celebrating the making of new wine; rituals also involved sacrifices.

3. Tragedies, satyr plays, and comedies were staged. The first Dionysia was celebrated by Athens about 534 B.C., when the tyrant Pisistratus instituted a competition among playwrights. The first winner of the tragic competition was Thespis, who reportedly created the first role for an actor by separating a single performer from the traditional choir.

4. Tragedy, introduced by Thespis, originally means "goat song," a reference to the goatskins worn by the choir or the chants during the goat sacrifice.

5. Thespis and other dramatists wrote tragedies committed to the spirit of Dionysus, but used myths about other gods and heroes as their primary subject matter.

6. Only one surviving tragedy has Dionysus as its leading character: Euripides's *Bacchants*, presenting him as an irresistible natural instinct, contrary to the comedy by Aristophanes, *Frogs*, in which he is portrayed as a good-natured drunk.

7. Dramatic presentations then were communal rituals including music and dance.

8. Aristotle defined *tragedy* in terms of the audience's emotional response: by having strong feelings aroused, the spectator is able to relieve or purge these emotions, achieving catharsis.

NOTE: While Aristotle was an avid defender of the moral value of the theater, his teacher Plato advised against letting one's emotions be affected by the dramatic arts. Plato saw the arts as a threat to a person's rational equilibrium, regardless of the fact that he himself wrote artful literature (the *Dialogues*) that affected his readers' emotions as well as their reason; the debate still exists today in the current discussion of whether certain art forms are harmful to the spectator, or whether they have a calming, cleansing effect. The debate about violence in films and on television has clear Aristotelian and Platonic overtones; however, it must be remembered that Aristotle, being the defender of the ideal of moderation, never intended for people to be exposed to drama on a daily basis; he believed that too much of a good thing was harmful.

54

9. The satyr play, following a series of three tragedies, used mythic material but did not take it seriously. The chorus, composed of satyrs, would tell obscene jokes and provoke laughter. Falling victim to Christian disapproval, most satyr plays have been lost.

10. The comedy was added to the Dionysia in Athens in 486 B.C. The comic festival, the Lenaea, was established about 440 B.C. Comedy began with the Dionysian band of revelers walking in procession, answering calls from the onlookers. *Komoidia* is derived from "parade of revelers."

11. Apollo encourages awareness of one's human limitations; however, the tragic hero has a capacity for extremes of feeling and behavior that contradicts this. The Dionysian drive toward self-exploration through freedom explores the urges that violate the taboos of civilized life.

12. In drama there is no narrative voice, so the characters may speak and act in ways that create several different perspectives on the occurring actions, leaving the audience to contemplate the possibilities.

13. Greek dramatists were expected to base their tragedies on myths, but they often questioned the traditional perspective of the myths.

14. The tragic protagonists are noble, as in the myths, but slightly more realistic: instead of tracing their descent from the gods, they are of noble families; and instead of performing superhuman feats, they are persons of unusual moral integrity.

15. The extraordinary qualities of the heroes are often what cause their predicaments—and their rise above those predicaments.

16. The tragic heroes are doomed to suffer, because they are trapped between conflicting demands. Their suffering ripples outward, affecting others, but their role is to take on the communal suffering, much like a scapegoat.

17. Through suffering they reach wisdom; the tragic quest is typically an internal journey of suffering and transcendence of suffering.

18. Those who are not strong enough to live through the suffering and reach wisdom die, like Oedipus's wife Jocasta.

19. The tragic universe is ruled by divine beings, but the universe is anthropocentric; the words of the gods are ambiguous, and there is little communication between them and humans. The humans keep struggling to confront the limits of the cosmic order.

20. The tragic universe is not morally neat; there is no assured divine justice and no moral clarity in the end. *Peripeteia* (reversal) defines the tragic experience.

21. Even if the gods are incomprehensible, the protagonist accepts responsibility for his or her fate; defining ourselves as free moral agents means acting as if we were free and responsible.

22. The final insight of the tragic hero corresponds loosely to the epiphany of the Dionysian ritual: as the drives are released, the order of the drama is restored, and the community survives. In this way Apollo and Dionysus are reconciled.

KEY NAMES OF MYTHOLOGICAL CHARACTERS MENTIONED

Dionysus

Apollo

Oedipus, king of Thebes

Jocasta, his wife and mother

Agamemnon, leader of the Greeks at Troy

Achilles, Greek hero of the siege of Troy

Antigone, daughter of Oedipus and Jocasta (and sister of Oedipus)

Orestes, son and slayer of Agamemnon

KEY NAMES ASSOCIATED WITH THE TELLING/CRITICISM OF MYTHS

Friedrich Nietzsche, German philosopher (1844–1900)

Thespis, the first Greek tragic dramatist (about 534 B.C.)

Euripides (c. 485–406 B.C.)

Aristophanes, Greek comic dramatist (c. 450–c. 380 B.C.)

Aeschylus (c. 525–456 B.C.)

Sophocles (c. 495–406 B.C.)

William Blake, English painter and poet (1757–1827)

CHAPTER 14

COSMIC CONFLICT AND EVOLUTION: AESCHYLUS'S TRANSFORMATION OF THE PROMETHEUS MYTH

MAIN POINTS

1. Hesiod's audience were farmers and petty magistrates; two hundred years later, the audience of Aeschylus was the population of Athens.

2. Aeschylus, a veteran, had fought at the Battle of Marathon helping Athens defeat a Persian force, and at Salamis where the Greeks' victory over the Persians was decisive.

3. After the Persian wars, Athens emerged as the leading city-state. The Athenians had established their democratic government twenty years before the Persian invasion.

4. Except for the comedies of Aristophanes, all Greek plays were written between the end of the Persian wars and the deaths of Sophocles and Euripides.

5. Aeschylus shaped tragedy into the dominant literary form of Greece's Golden Age, c. 480–404 B.C. His oldest surviving play may be *Persians* (c. 472 B.C.), one of the few based on contemporary history.

6. Most regard *Prometheus Bound* as written by Aeschylus. While borrowing the subject from Hesiod, he changes Prometheus into a heroic rebel and makes Zeus a tyrant.

7. The image of Zeus was radically different from what the audience was used to; Aeschylus also presents him as neither omnipotent nor omniscient—and vulnerable to fatal error.

8. *Prometheus Bound* is the first part of a trilogy; the other two parts, *Prometheus Unbound* and *Prometheus the Fire-Bearer,* remain only in fragments.

9. Aeschylus follows the tradition in which Zeus allows Heracles to kill the eagle feasting on Prometheus's liver; in Aeschylus's interpretation this leads to a reconciliation between Zeus and Prometheus, in effect restaging Zeus's swallowing of Metis to assimilate her qualities.

10. The first part of the trilogy casts divine power against divine intelligence: Zeus versus Prometheus. The play opens with Prometheus being immobilized on the rock.

11. Prometheus admits to have helped humans because he has compassion for their suffering.

12. The poet Shelley interpreted Prometheus as an image of the human mind, remaining free despite its physical bondage.

13. From the human viewpoint Prometheus is a savior; from Zeus's perspective he is a lawbreaker. This reflects the Greek ambivalence toward an individualism that may disrupt social order.

NOTE: The punishment of Prometheus has a parallel in the story of the Norse trickster god Loki; however, Prometheus's crime is committed for the benefit of humanity, while Loki mainly looks out for himself. Son of the ancient giants (*jätter*, in some ways comparable to the Titans), Loki's main function seems to have been to aggravate the Aesir in any way possible, including telling them truths about themselves that they did not want to hear, although he is also represented as Odin's travel companion and an occasional helper of the other gods. Loki transgresses against the gods, either by causing the death of the god Balder, or by breaking up a party by slandering the gods (an older tradition); after a long chase he is caught and chained to a rock; as chains the gods use the intestines of one of his sons, killed by another son as part of his punishment. Above his head the gods place a poisonous snake with venom dripping onto his face; his faithful wife Sigyn remains by his side, catching the venom in a bowl, but every time she has to empty the bowl the venom drips on Loki's face, causing him to shake in agony; that is the Norse explanation of earthquakes. Scholars have pointed out the mythological parallels between other trickster gods such as the Native American Coyote and the Ossetic trickster Syrdon, and some have pointed out that the "bound giant" may be a very ancient mythological theme. Christian monks collecting the Norse myths seem to have given Loki particularly diabolic traits to create a parallel between him and the devil.

---

14. Hesiod claims Prometheus is a second-generation Titan; Aeschylus identifies him as a son of Gaea.

15. The chorus of the play charges that Prometheus misses the mark of wise self-interest, displaying hubris.

16. The play's Prometheus is the last free mind in the universe to distinguish between good and evil; his virtue of intellectual honesty brings about his suffering.

17. A character's tragic error is *hamartia*, to "miss the mark." It can apply to any action which fails in hitting the target of divine approval.

18. Two scenes help convey Aeschylus's interpretation of Prometheus: the young woman Io being stung by a gadfly sent by Hera, victimized because of Zeus's lust for her.

19. In the climactic episode, the chorus sides with Prometheus against Hermes and Zeus, although the Greek chorus usually takes a mediating position. Thus the audience is asked to choose to support principle over power.

20. Prometheus's defiance gives Zeus an opportunity to save himself from a future downfall at the hands of a stronger son. In his turn, Prometheus is liberated when Chiron wants to die to escape suffering. In dying, Chiron vicariously atones for Prometheus's offense.

21. Because of an oath sworn by Zeus that he wouldn't release Prometheus, Prometheus must wear a fragment of the rock attached to a steel ring.

PRIMARY TEXT SELECTION: Aeschylus, *Prometheus Bound*

KEY NAMES OF MYTHOLOGICAL CHARACTERS MENTIONED

Zeus

Prometheus

Heracles

Chiron, the wise centaur

Io, Zeus's lover, punished by Hera by being transformed into a cow, stung by a gadfly

Hermes, messenger of the gods

KEY NAMES ASSOCIATED WITH THE TELLING/CRITICISM OF MYTHS

Hesiod (eighth century B.C.)

Aeschylus (c. 525–456 B.C.)

Percy Bysshe Shelley, English poet (1792–1822)

CHAPTER 15

THE HOUSE OF ATREUS: AESCHYLUS'S *ORESTEIA*

MAIN POINTS

1. Aeschylus's *Oresteia*, the only surviving Greek trilogy, examines the courses and consequences of the murder of Agamemnon by his wife, Clytemnestra, and the subsequent dilemma facing their son Orestes.

2. Orestes affords the gods an opportunity to redefine the nature of justice and divinity.

3. The evolutionary change in the human and divine spheres is Aeschylus's main concern; this change will unite opposites.

4. As in the *Prometheus* trilogy, Aeschylus explores the Greek belief that the gods are not unchangeable but, instead, grow into ethical maturity with the passing of time.

5. The *Oresteia* shows the influence of human society on Zeus's moral evolution.

6. In the third part (the *Eumenides*), the Furies are transformed into protectors; thus a moral revolution has taken place, shifting from personal vendetta to the institution of the court of law.

7. The first play, the *Agamemnon*, opens in Argos shortly before Agamemnon's return from Troy. The second play, the *Libation-Bearers*, takes place after Orestes has returned from exile several years later. The third play, the *Eumenides*, features Orestes seeking purification at Delphi.

8. From Argos to Athens, the theme shifts from vengeance to justice and ethics; the climax is the transformation of the Furies.

9. Aeschylus also created a satyr play based on an episode in the *Odyssey*: Menelaus's encounter with Proteus.

10. The chorus of the *Agamemnon* is composed of older citizens of Argos, reduced to onlookers, even when the Trojan princess Cassandra describes her visions of Agamemnon's impending murder.

11. The chorus of the *Libation-Bearers* are captive Trojan women honoring the slain Agamemnon and hating his queen.

12. The chorus of the *Eumenides* are the Furies, half-sisters of Aphrodite, ancient chthonic powers opposing the ouranic deities of Olympus. The Furies punish crimes against blood kin.

13. The father of Agamemnon and Menelaus, Atreus, inherits a proclivity toward evil from his ancestor Tantalus, serving his son's dismembered body as food for the gods; the act is repeated by Atreus in a feud with his brother.

14. Before leaving Argos for Troy, Agamemnon sacrifices his daughter Iphigenia to the gods for a fair wind to Troy, responding to the pressures of his soldiers.

15. At the fall of Troy, Agamemnon desecrates the city's shrines and abducts the virgin priestess of Apollo, the princess Cassandra.

16. Apollo gave Cassandra clairvoyance, but when she rebuffed his attempts at seduction, he put the curse on her that nobody would believe her prophecies.

17. Before her own murder, Cassandra throws down her prophet's emblems, a victim of the brutality of both humans and gods.

18. The *Agamemnon* confronts Agamemnon with his wife, who has been ruling Argos in his absence; Clytemnestra dares her husband to commit hubris, taking on an honor for himself reserved for the gods by walking on the carpet-covered steps.

19. She kills him in the bath, taking credit for the regicide, since she believes herself to be an instrument of justice. Her lover, Aegisthus, takes no part in the killing.

20. In spite of apparently representing matriarchal rights in her grieving for Iphigenia, Clytemnestra shows no solidarity toward other women nor even any affection toward her younger daughter, Electra.

21. Clytemnestra is a strong female character of the trilogy, embodying the question for the Greek community of how to deal with a powerful and intelligent woman. The play suggests that such a woman cannot be trusted.

22. In the *Libation-Bearers,* Orestes has to decide whether to obey Apollo's order to avenge his father by slaying his mother, which means he would incur the wrath of the Furies, who will claim his life and his soul.

23. Orestes's friend Pylades repeats Apollo's command, and Orestes kills his mother; afterwards he feels anguish at seeing the Furies, which nobody else can see.

24. In the prologue of the *Eumenides,* the Pythia reminds us that a succession of earth goddesses presided at Delphi prior to Apollo, signifying a shift from chthonic to ouranic powers.

25. In the trial scene of the *Eumenides* binary tensions become pronounced.

26. The female principle is identified with the forces of darkness, whereas the male powers for Aeschylus stand for clemency, light, and moderation.

27. This identification of the female principle reaches a peak when Apollo declares that a mother is merely an incubator for the seed that the father deposits in her; as an example he cites Athene, produced without the aid of a woman. Legally, only a male has parental status.

28. This identification also serves to associate Athene with the masculine principle, and accordingly, she sides with male authority.

29. Aeschylus's primary interest in the third play is the change of the Furies into benign beings, based on conditions set up throughout the play.

30. In the *Oresteia*, the opposing aspects of divinity, the Furies and the Olympians, are merged into a harmonious whole by a democratic act of persuasion, as the Furies become the Eumenides, the Kindly Ones.

31. Transformed, these spirits now perform stabilizing social functions.

32. Prior to Aeschylus, the story of Agamemnon and Orestes usually illustrated a competition for power between male figures. In the Homeric version it is Aegisthus, not Clytemnestra, who kills Agamemnon.

33. In the *Eumenides,* all the principal characters are used to illustrate polar opposites, mediated by Athene to achieve harmony; this use of myth lends itself to a structuralist interpretation.

34. For Aeschylus the ancient Mycenaean legacy has evolved into a new concept of social justice that finds completion in the Athenian court of law.

35. Other poets have created sequels to the *Oresteia* that tell about Orestes's subsequent adventures. Euripides's play, *Iphigenia in Tauris*, reunites Orestes and his sister.

36. In another version of the Orestes myth, he abducts the daughter of Helen and Menelaus, originally engaged to be married to him but married off to Neoptolemus. Eventually he succeeds both Agamemnon and Menelaus, uniting the kingdoms of Argos and Sparta and founding new colonies on the sites of the cities destroyed in the Trojan War, thus putting an end to the violence of the House of Atreus.

NOTE: In the *Eumenides,* the ghost of Clytemnestra appears, reproaching the Furies for not being able to find Orestes and avenge her, and spurring them on to hunt Orestes down. As Clytemnestra evoked matriarchal rights earlier, so, too, does this aspect of her carry elements of the Great Goddess, in the form of Hecate. Hecate is often depicted as the leader of the Wild Hunt, a phantom chase of riders and dogs (usually consisting of the souls of the dead) across the night skies. The myth of the Wild Hunt is known in many traditions from Malay to Celtic folklore; among the most well-known leaders of the Wild Hunt in European folklore are King Arthur and Odin.

KEY NAMES OF MYTHOLOGICAL CHARACTERS MENTIONED

Agamemnon, leader of the Greek army at Troy

Clytemnestra, his wife

Orestes, their son

Electra, their daughter

Iphigenia, their daughter, sacrificed at Aulis

Aegisthus, Clytemnestra's lover

Cassandra, a Trojan priestess, captured by Agamemnon

Atreus, the father of Agamemnon and Menelaus

Tantalus, their ancestor

Apollo

Furies (the Erinyes), nighttime spirits of vengeance

Eumenides, the Kindly Ones, the Furies after their transformation

KEY NAMES ASSOCIATED WITH THE TELLING/CRITICISM OF MYTHS

Aeschylus (c. 525–456 B.C.)

Homer (ninth century B.C.)

Euripides (c. 485–406 B.C.)

CHAPTER 16

THE TRAGIC HERO: SOPHOCLES'S OEDIPUS

MAIN POINTS

1. Sophocles lived through the classical age of Greece, witnessing the development of democracy, the political rise of Athens, and achievements of philosophers, artists, writers, and mathematicians.

2. The Peloponnesian War shattered many illusions, but even prior to the beginning of the war (431 B.C.) the rapid cultural changes caused people to reexamine their traditional perspectives on the world order.

3. Sophocles's tragedies reflect this transitional time of reevaluation of the role of the gods, coinciding with cultural progress.

4. Sophocles participated in public life, held various offices, and wrote more than 125 plays of which seven have survived.

5. Three of these plays are about Oedipus, but they are not a trilogy. The first, *Antigone*, is the last in the narrative sequence, dealing with Oedipus's daughter Antigone's martyrdom.

6. *Oedipus Rex*, probably written between 429 and 425 B.C., speaks to a plague-weary Athens about the plague in Thebes.

7. Sigmund Freud argued that *Oedipus Rex* is relevant because every male child unconsciously desires to kill his father and marry his mother; the repression of these urges gives rise to the Oedipus complex.

8. Sophocles anticipates Freudian themes: Jocasta believes that appalling urges are common and are revealed in dreams, and that these urges must be repressed. Oedipus's own endeavor to find the truth can be compared with the psychoanalytic process.

9. Two forms of failure of knowledge produce illness: the people's indifference to the murderer of their king, and Oedipus's ignorance of his own identity. His discovery of the truth has cathartic effects.

NOTE: It may be relevant to ask whether Oedipus himself suffered from an Oedipus complex; in Freud's scenario, the young male child of the nuclear family is attracted to his mother and is jealous of his father monopolizing her; unconsciously he wants to get his father out of the way but worries about his father's punishment, a fear translated into the fear of castration. Oedipus, having been told by the Oracle at Delphi that he will kill his father and marry his mother, refuses to go home to Corinth for as long as they are alive, because he doesn't want to risk placing himself or them in such a situation; the man he ends up killing is a stranger to him, and so is the woman he marries. It is debatable how well the actual story of Oedipus reflects what Freud refers to as the Oedipus complex.

---

10. Apollo is the one calling attention to the conditions through his oracle; so is Apollo decreeing the fate of Oedipus, or is he merely foreseeing it? Does Oedipus have freedom of the will, or is his life predetermined?

11. Apollo, as controller of fate, announces that the city of Thebes will suffer from the plague until the king's murderer has been exiled.

12. The series of coincidences also point to fate controlling human experience.

13. Tiresias also validates the oracle's authority. Being blind, he has the gift of inner sight, undistracted by surface appearances or gender restrictions.

14. The myths about Oedipus's family refer to a curse, but Sophocles never alludes to that.

15. The sin that angers Apollo is not Oedipus's murder and incest, but the lack of civic duty displayed by the citizens of Thebes.

16. Thebes had a reputation for evil and was an enemy of Athens, having sided with the Persians and having fought the Athenians during the Peloponnesian War. The Theban people are punished by the plague.

17. Oedipus's own punishment, blinding himself, exceeds the exile demanded by Apollo.

18. Both the acts of Laius exposing his child and the acts of Oedipus leaving Corinth are intended to preempt the will of the gods, but instead they help bring it about.

19. Father and son make similar behavioral choices, determined by pride and anger; when Oedipus is angry, his reason does not prevail; he may not have inherited curses from his father but personality traits.

20. Riddles are essential to the story; Oedipus's intelligence in solving the Sphinx's riddle makes his marriage to Jocasta possible.

21. The riddle of the Sphinx: What creature walks on four legs in the morning, two legs in the afternoon, and three legs in the evening? A human being.

22. Oedipus solves the riddle but fails to see its significance: Only for a short time in midlife are humans in relative control of their lives.

23. Human beings are riddles to themselves and not in control of their psyches, where shadow selves are hiding.

24. *Oedipus Rex* raises metaphysical questions such as: Why do terrible things happen to good people? Do humans have a destiny—or a choice?

25. In the end, Oedipus accepts that there is no answer and that human logic can't explain the intentions of the gods.

26. He furthermore takes responsibility for his actions, even though he acted out of ignorance, and this leaves him free. When Oedipus accepts his role as a scapegoat, the plague is lifted from Thebes.

27. By putting his eyes out, Oedipus becomes a parallel to Tiresias with his inner sight, the awareness of truth.

28. Oedipus goes through a personal journey to an inner hell and returns; he is both hero and victim, freed by his own experience.

29. In Sophocles's last play, written twenty-five years later, Oedipus is on the road to Colonus where tradition claims he was buried; *Oedipus at Colonus* has slightly different details than *Oedipus Rex*.

30. Oedipus's sons have taken over the government from Creon; despite their quarrel they want their father back in Thebes, because according to the oracle the city which earns Oedipus's goodwill will prosper after he is dead.

31. Sophocles's Athenian audience would relate well to the praise of Athens at the expense of Thebes.

32. Similarities between the two plays include Oedipus still carrying the burden of his sins as well as his continued anger. But in *Oedipus Rex* he took responsibility for his acts, whereas in *Oedipus at Colonus* he insists on his innocence and victimization by the gods.

33. No longer self-sufficient, he has learned patience and suffers loneliness.

34. In *Oedipus at Colonus,* opposites are reconciled in a series of paradoxes; Oedipus becomes an avenger himself, and blinded he sees the truth of the mystery and is reconciled with the gods.

35. In *Oedipus Rex,* Oedipus rejects the feminine principle; in the last play he embraces this principle by entering the sacred grove of the Furies (the Eumenides), who accept him.

NOTE: According to the mythologist Robert Graves, there may have been a historical King Oedipus; he may not have killed his father and married his mother, but he may have been the consort of a priestess-queen. Graves speculates that this event may have marked the transition between Goddess worship and patriarchal rule; Oedipus may have been one of a series of consort-kings, temporary sacrificial husbands (often referred to as sons) of the priestess-queen representing the Great Goddess, but refusing to be sacrificed as tradition demanded, thus establishing a patriarchal kingdom and causing the downfall of the priestess-rule.

---

36. Oedipus finally experiences death and transfiguration, becoming deified; like the Furies, he has become one of the Kindly Ones.

37. The earliest of Sophocles's plays is the last in the narrative sequence; *Antigone* takes place after Oedipus and his two sons are dead and Creon is again in power.

38. Polynices, who attacked Athens, is left unburied, an act of impiety. Antigone argues that the gods are a higher authority than the state and attempts to bury him herself.

39. Antigone is arrested and buried alive in a cave; when Creon relents at the advice of Tiresias and opens the cave, she has hanged herself, and her fiancé, Creon's son, takes his own life. So does Creon's wife, his mother.

> **PRIMARY TEXT SELECTION:** Sophocles, *Opedipus Rex, Oedipus at Colonus*

KEY NAMES OF MYTHOLOGICAL CHARACTERS MENTIONED

Oedipus, king of Thebes

Jocasta, his wife and birth mother

Laius, former king of Thebes, Jocasta's husband, Oedipus's father

Antigone, their daughter

Ismene, their daughter

Eteocles, their son

Polynices, their son

Creon, Jocasta's brother

Polybus of Corinth, Oedipus's foster father

Dorian Merope, his foster mother

Apollo

Tiresias, the blind seer

Theseus, Greek hero, ruler of Athens

KEY NAMES ASSOCIATED WITH THE TELLING/CRITICISM OF MYTHS

Sophocles (c. 495–406 B.C.)

Sigmund Freud (1856–1939)

CHAPTER 17

EURIPIDES'S *MEDEA:*
A DIFFERENT PERSPECTIVE ON TRAGEDY

MAIN POINTS

1. Euripides was considered an eccentric and an intellectual radical.

2. His plays were sometimes considered too strange and offensive for the taste of the conservative Athenian audience.

3. *Medea* (431 B.C.) stresses the female perspective: Medea has given up everything for Jason; her reward is to have him desert her for a younger, richer, and prettier woman, a princess.

4. Jason denies Medea's role in helping him and wants to deprive her of her role as mother of their children, too.

5. Medea has all the strengths of the tragic hero: the intensity, the commitment, and the heroic acts. The chorus implies that motherhood is heroic in itself.

6. Medea believes that her gods, Hecate, Themis, and Zeus, are with her in her fury against Jason; he is a breaker of oaths and deserves punishment, but it is the princess and the children who are made to suffer.

7. The play opens with Medea engaging in a last-ditch attempt to use rhetoric, not violence. Jason is incapable of listening; in language as in life, he confuses style with substance.

8. Medea announces openly her plans and acknowledges the deed afterwards.

9. Medea is a passionate woman, driven by irrational forces to hurt the ones she loves.

10. Euripides uses the capacity of the drama to present multiple points of view, shifting angles to make a different perspective appear.

11. While most other female protagonists pay the price for their crimes in Greek tragedies, Medea escapes punishment by going to Athens where King Aegeus gives her refuge.

12. In contrast to most other dramas, Medea's murder is described in detail onstage.

13. In Euripides's plays, the common people provide an important perspective, such as the women of Corinth in *Medea* who make moral distinctions.

14. The nurse in *Medea* advocates moderation as self-control and comments on the perversity of a self-indulgent upper class.

15. Medea and Jason belong to the upper class, but they are dispossessed; they are depicted at home, and not on some adventure; their problems are monetary, not metaphysical; in *Medea,* the heroes act like ordinary people.

16. Medea is the one who comes closest to the suffering protagonist of the Greek drama.

17. Jason will not acknowledge his complicity in Medea's crimes and is revealed as a coward who uses women for his own gain. His death is unheroic, being struck on the head by a beam while asleep on his ship.

18. In traditional tragedies important people commit appalling deeds, and their passions as well as their violence are portrayed nobly. In *Medea* Euripides shows us the inhuman brutality of the murder by describing it in detail; the violence is not ennobling, but merely sadistic.

19. If this is what heroes are like, then perhaps we should admire the common people.

20. Tragedy takes place in an unpredictable universe where the tragic protagonist may suffer disproportionately; Euripides explores the converse idea that the wicked may also prosper, as in *Electra* where the daughter who slays Clytemnestra lives happily ever after.

21. In *Electra* Euripides incorporates parody, spoofing Aeschylus's recognition scene between the siblings Electra and Orestes.

22. In *Medea* he mocks the traditional tragic vision of the heroic values of ancient myth.

23. In the play's final speech, the chorus comments on the unreliability of the gods. There is no sign of divine acceptance; no gods provide Medea with symbolic sanctions.

24. When Medea taunts Jason with the notion that he thinks the old gods no longer prevail, she may be referring to an older generation of chthonic gods such as Hecate who have taken over.

25. If so, we are back in an amoral universe of vengeance where irrational forces prevail.

26. Though Athens was a city of justice and equality, it oppressed its women, just as Jason did. With the preparations for the war with Sparta, perhaps the Athenians were receptive to Euripides's vision of the world gone mad.

PRIMARY TEXT SELECTION: Euripides, *Medea*

KEY NAMES OF MYTHOLOGICAL CHARACTERS MENTIONED

Medea, sorceress daughter of King Aeetes of Colchis, wife of Jason

Jason, Greek adventurer who brought back the Golden Fleece

Aegeus, king of Athens, Theseus's father

Electra, Orestes's sister, Agamemnon and Clytemnestra's daughter

KEY NAMES ASSOCIATED WITH THE TELLING/CRITICISM OF MYTHS

Euripides (c. 485–406 B.C.)

CHAPTER 18

TRIUMPH OF THE IRRATIONAL: EURIPIDES'S *BACCHANTS*

MAIN POINTS

1. Euripides's *Bacchants*, written about fifty-two years after Aeschylus's *Oresteia*, tears down the Apollonian order in the portrayal of Dionysus establishing his cult in Thebes.

2. Under Dionysus's influence the women of Thebes have fled to the hills where they commune with nature.

3. Proliferation of miracles and natural signs characterizes the play and strengthens the faith of Dionysus's worshipers, but also the resistance among his skeptics.

4. King Pentheus believes the cult will reduce his city-state to chaos, but he destroys himself and his family by not recognizing his kinship with the powers that Dionysus stands for.

5. Euripides wrote the *Bacchants* in Macedonia where he witnessed the cult's rituals in the wild and may have seen in the myth an image of the destructive passions of the contemporary Greek culture.

6. Athenian civilization was deteriorating due to the war with Sparta.

7. The *Bacchants* is named for its two choruses, Asian female devotees of Dionysus and Theban women of the cult.

8. Pentheus is the son of Agave and Echion, one of the Spartoi men created from dragon's teeth by Cadmus, the founder of Thebes.

9. The cousin of Dionysus and a descendant of the Goddess's serpent (the dragon), Pentheus should recognize Dionysus's divinity, but he fails to perceive those qualities in himself.

10. When Dionysus appears disguised as a young stranger, Pentheus humiliates him in public and condemns him as morally soft.

11. Pentheus is afraid of what may happen if human nature is liberated from its socially imposed restraints, such as the unleashing of the female libido.

12. Agave fulfills her son's deepest fears in her divine possession: she proves the equal of any male Theban soldier but forfeits her maternal identity in her destructive passion.

13. Agave's realization that she is carrying Pentheus's severed head is one of the most powerful *anagnorisis* (recognition) scenes in all drama.

14. With her sanity returning, Agave sees that Dionysus has violated her integrity, and in the end she rejects Dionysus and returns to her former identity, but being a kin-slayer, she is not allowed to join her son in death.

15. The rejection of divine possession echoes that of Cassandra in the *Agamemnon*: union with a god is seen as depriving them of personal autonomy. Both refuse to submit completely and are punished by the gods.

16. In the play's major *peripateia* (reversal), Pentheus and Dionysus change places: Pentheus, the king and soldier, is transformed into his feminine self, revealing his anxiety about his sexual identity.

17. Dionysus condemns Pentheus to die as a transvestite voyeur, torn to pieces by the women on whom he came to spy; he himself becomes the ritual sacrifice, reenacting Dionysus's own sparagmos.

18. Dionysus changes his physical shape to reveal his divine-animal nature, embodying the ethical contradictions intrinsic to nature.

19. Tiresias accepts Dionysus as divine with no hesitation and advises Pentheus to do likewise, claiming that humanity benefits equally from grain and wine. He successfully balances the unavoidable contrarieties of control and freedom.

20. Euripides's audience would have been familiar with Tiresias's ability to assimilate opposites in his personal history of having been changed to a woman and back to a man.

21. Tiresias's accommodation of both Apollo and Dionysus parallels Delphi's accommodation of the two forces in one site, honoring the principle of irrationality by giving it limited expression.

22. Cadmus's acceptance of Dionysus is superficial, and consequently he is condemned by Dionysus to exile and transformation into a snake.

23. The triumphant Dionysus is incapable of pity, being an aspect of nature that transcends moral judgment; sympathy is a human response to tragic loss, but the god is above such feelings.

24. Agave observes that gods should be ethically superior to humans; this wish may be vain when applied to Dionysian passions.

PRIMARY TEXT SELECTION: Euripides, *Bacchants*

KEY NAMES OF MYTHOLOGICAL CHARACTERS MENTIONED

Dionysus

Pentheus, king of Thebes

Agave, his mother, Semele's sister

Semele, Dionysus's mother

Echion, his father, one of the Spartoi

Spartoi, men created from dragon's teeth by Cadmus

Cadmus, the founder of Thebes, Agave's father

Europa, his sister, abducted by Zeus

Tiresias

KEY NAMES ASSOCIATED WITH THE TELLING/CRITICISM OF MYTHS

Euripides (c. 485–406 B.C.)

CHAPTER 19

PLATO'S USE OF MYTHOLOGY

MAIN POINTS

1. The wars between Athens and Sparta heightened the contrast between rational practice of moderation and emotional excesses.

2. The Oracle at Delphi pronounced that no one in Greece was wiser than Socrates and Euripides, who both advocated temperance.

3. Socrates employed the method of publicly asking government officials how they could prove the validity of their policies. He devoted much of his career to search for absolute values; it eventually brought him into conflict with state authorities who tried, convicted, and executed him.

4. Plato, Socrates's student, saw Socrates as the ideal "lover of wisdom" and made him the chief speaker in most of his dialogues.

5. To Plato, philosophy was an Apollonian discipline that illuminated the dual nature of reality: the physical world, being in constant flux, is unknowable, whereas the spiritual world of forms is real and unchanging.

6. The soul originates in heaven and is immortal, but it is trapped in a physical body.

7. Although rational, Plato's philosophy is also intuitive and infused with the emotional power of myth; in this way Plato could give his readers images of a reality inaccessible to logical analysis.

8. He was critical of Homeric myth but utilized revised myths in his teachings.

9. The dialogue the *Republic* describes a utopian state consisting of three distinct classes of citizens and closes with the "Myth of Er." (See Note, p. 76.)

10. The "Allegory of the Cave" illustrates the soul's earthly imprisonment; we are like prisoners in a cave who mistake shadows for realities. Philosophy helps us escape and glimpse the true reality of the spiritual dimension.

11. The "Myth of Er" illustrates the soul's fate after death; after Er is killed in battle, his soul travels to the region where souls are judged and witnesses the process of reincarnation by choice; having cultivated spiritual values in life, souls can make careful choices.

12. The gods are not responsible for human folly or wickedness; each soul freely adopts its destiny.

13. There are elements of the cults of Dionysus, Orpheus, and Demeter in this account, but they are transformed by Plato's Apollonian vision of divine wisdom and justice.

14. Virgil's *Aeneid* embellishes on the Platonic superiority of spirit to flesh; the Sibyl of Delphi initiates the hero into the mysteries of the spirit world.

NOTE: Plato's *Republic* serves as a blueprint not only for his utopian society but also for a normative psychology of the soul trapped in a body. Plato describes the soul as being tripartite, consisting of a lower part (appetites), a middle part (willpower, or passion), and a higher part (reason). In the dialogue *Phaedrus,* he tells a fable about the internal relationships among the three parts: They are like a charioteer and two horses. One horse is undisciplined; the other is well behaved, and the charioteer has to make the best of this uneven couple. With the help of the well-behaved horse (willpower), the charioteer (reason) must control the unruly horse (appetites), because without willpower, reason has no practical control over desires, and without reason, willpower has no direction. In the same manner Plato, in the *Republic,* envisions the perfect and just society as a tripartite structure consisting of the merchants and farmers (appetites), the auxiliaries (willpower), and the philosopher-kings (reason). As philosophers and political thinkers have often commented, this translates into a totalitarian society in which the people at the bottom of the system are under complete control by the soldiers (auxiliaries) and the rulers, even though the philosopher-kings are supposed to be benevolent rulers.

15. The radical split between physical nature and immaterial soul greatly influenced early Christianity. The "Myth of Er" anticipates popular Judeo-Christian beliefs about the afterlife.

16. In the dialogue the *Symposium,* Plato gives a humorous account of the origin of the sexes. In the dialogue Aristophanes offers an etiological myth; in the beginning humans were round, had two heads, and had two sets of arms and legs. There were three sexes, one all male, one all female, and one androgynous. Punished by Zeus for their ambition and challenging of the gods, Zeus split them in two. Since then, humans have been searching for their lost counterpart.

17. The dialogues the *Timaeus* and the *Critias* contain the myth of Atlantis, a highly advanced civilization in the Atlantic Ocean that vanished overnight as a result of its hubris.

18. Modern geologists speculate that the legend could be a dim memory of the Minoan city located on Thera, destroyed in the volcanic eruption in 1628 B.C.

KEY NAMES OF MYTHOLOGICAL CHARACTERS MENTIONED

Er, a native of Pamphylia killed in battle

Ardiaeus, a despot of Pamphylia, punished in the afterlife

Lachesis, Clotho, and Atropos, the three Fates

Orpheus, husband of Eurydice, founder of Orphism

Ajax, a Greek warrior at Troy

Agamemnon

Atalanta, a runner

Epeius, maker of the Trojan Horse

Odysseus

KEY NAMES ASSOCIATED WITH THE TELLING/CRITICISM OF MYTHS

Euripides (c. 485–406 B.C.)

Socrates (c. 469–399 B.C.)

Plato (c. 427–347 B.C.)

Aristophanes, Greek comic dramatist (c. 450–c. 380 B.C.)

CHAPTER 20

THE ROMAN VISION:
GREEK MYTHS AND ROMAN REALITIES

MAIN POINTS

1. Roman culture, including Roman mythology, often borrows elements from other cultures such as the Etruscans and the Greeks.

2. The Roman emperor Augustus boasted that he had transformed Rome into a city of marble; the reconstruction did not involve demolition, however, but adding false-front marble columns to brick buildings.

3. The Romans, feeling culturally inferior to the Greeks, had adopted Greek literature and mythology, while changing names and adapting the concepts to fit their ideas and values.

4. Through the works of Roman writers such as Virgil and Ovid, classical mythology was transmitted to the later Western culture.

5. According to the myth of Romulus and Remus, Rhea Silvia was assigned to the office of Vestal Virgin by her uncle Amulius, a usurper to the throne who hoped to prevent her from producing heirs. Seduced by Mars she bore twin sons, Romulus and Remus.

6. Amulius set the infants adrift in a basket, but they survived and were nursed by a she-wolf. When adult, they restored their father to the throne of his city, Alba Longa.

NOTE: Worldwide, myths about the birth and upbringing of culture heroes include stories about the child being put in a basket and set adrift on the waters of the river or the ocean, usually in order to save the child's life from persecutors; however, such stories also reflect a common custom of exposing unwanted babies, placing them in the hands of the gods. In the Judeo-Christian tradition the story of Moses is the most familiar one. The Norse and German tradition tells of Siegfried (Sigurd) whose mother placed him in a glass vessel, which accidentally fell in the river; the boy arrived safely on an island in the ocean where a doe nursed him along with her young. The Hindu tradition tells of Kunti, who threw her son into the river where he was rescued by a charioteer who raised the boy as his own, calling him Vasusena, later known for his great generosity. The Polynesian god Maui was born prematurely, and his mother Taranga cast him into the sea to prevent him from becoming an evil spirit; the sea deities preserved the child and put him ashore where he was discovered and raised by his ancestor Tama'rangi. Other children exposed—on mountains, not on the river—include Cybele and Oedipus. The release of the child into the river may represent a return to the protection of the Great Goddess and also a purification ritual; the hero loses ties with his original parents, is often nursed by animals representing nature, and is reborn to a unique existence.

78

7. Romulus and Remus later fought over which of them their own city should be named after; Remus was killed, and the city founded was named Rome.

8. The men who joined Romulus were without women, so he prepared a festival, inviting the residents of neighboring cities, including the Sabines. The Romans abducted and raped the daughters of the Sabines and later married them.

9. The Sabines warred against the Romans until the Romans' wives assured their families that they were content; the Roman and Sabine territories were combined, and Romulus ruled for thirty-eight years until his disappearance during a storm.

10. The myth of Romulus and Remus focuses on the city and its origins, and although it begins with mythic components, it quickly moves into actual history.

11. The myth's perspective is patriarchal; there is no trace of a feminine perspective left in the rape of Rhea Silvia and the Sabine women, contrary to similar Greek myths.

12. The abduction of Helen is a violation of the gods' will, and the centaurs' attempted rape of the Lapith women is punished by the gods; in contrast, the Romans are rewarded for similar behaviors.

13. Roman myth has fewer fantastic components than Greek myth; Thebes is founded by Cadmus sowing dragon's teeth, which turn into an army of men; the armed men of Rome are disgruntled farmers, shepherds, runaway slaves, and criminals.

14. Plutarch suggests a demythologizing explanation of the divine conception of the twins—a rape by Rhea Silvia's uncle.

15. Plutarch likewise demythologizes the myth of Theseus and the Minotaur.

16. Horace also reinterprets Greek mythology in a realistic vein, seeing Zeus's appearance to Danae as a shower of gold as an image of bribery.

17. The Romans create a Greek connection by having Romulus be fathered by Mars (Ares) and by having his mother be a descendant of Aeneas of Troy, himself a son of Aphrodite.

18. The Romans took over the body of Greek mythology but refocused the myths, historicized them, politicized them, and reinterpreted them to reflect Roman ideals.

19. The Roman pantheon is less dominated by abstractions than by practical concerns; Ceres becomes more important than Apollo and Minerva.

20. Hestia is unimportant in the Greek pantheon but as Vesta becomes the central symbol of Eternal Rome.

21. The Romans trace their ancestry to Mars, whereas the Greek attitude toward Ares is ambivalent.

22. Whereas Greek myths may be loosely based on historical events, Roman mythology is tied to real names, places, and events. Thus, Julius Caesar and Augustus trace their ancestry to Aeneas's son, Ascanius, nicknamed Ilus (Iulus).

23. Roman works of art, like Trajan's column, were intended to instruct as well as delight; the more grounded in reality the myths were, the better they could perform their didactic function.

24. Myths were also used to justify contemporary political realities, illustrating the secondary character of private emotions and worship compared to public duty.

25. In the home Romans worshiped the Lares, guardian spirits, the Penates, spirits of the pantry, and the Vesta, goddess of the hearth; their public counterparts were Jupiter, Juno, and Ceres. In domestic life the Romans paid service to the state itself.

26. Whereas the gods of Greece were largely apolitical and of no specific place, the Roman gods were exclusively Roman, predetermining Roman destiny.

27. The open-ended dynamic universe of Greek myth gives way to a teleological, goal-oriented Roman mythology of patriotism.

28. In order to maintain their ideal of the Pax Romana, the Romans had to rely on civic duty as a virtue, and patriotism became a survival tool. Defiance of the gods of Rome thus constituted treason as well as impiety.

29. From the gods' perspective all events were part of a divine plan; such a universe recognized no tragedy, only history incompletely understood.

30. The ego-driven Greek hero was too self-centered for Romans. The Roman hero had to exemplify the ideal Roman soldier and citizen.

31. Three early Roman qualities were essential: gravitas, pietas, and frugalitas.

32. Duty also requires the hero to control his passionate excesses so that his life and death can contribute to the triumph of Eternal Rome. Such a hero will be rewarded in the Underworld.

KEY NAMES OF MYTHOLOGICAL CHARACTERS MENTIONED

Rhea Silvia, the mother of Romulus and Remus

Amulius, her wicked uncle

Numitor, her father, the rightful ruler of Alba Longa

Helen, Menelaus's wife, abducted to Troy by Paris

Centaurs, half-horse, half-human creatures

Mars, the Roman god of war (Ares)

Aeneas, warrior of Troy, Romulus's ancestor

Jupiter (Zeus)

Juno (Hera)

Ceres (Demeter)

Minerva (Athene)

Vesta, the virgin protector of the hearth (Hestia)

KEY NAMES ASSOCIATED WITH THE TELLING/CRITICISM OF MYTHS

Virgil, Roman poet (70–19 B.C.)

Ovid, Roman poet (43 B.C.–17 A.D.)

Plutarch, Greek biographer (c. A.D. 46–120)

Horace, Roman poet (65–8 B.C.)

CHAPTER 21

THE *AENEID*: VIRGIL'S ROMAN EPIC

MAIN POINTS

1. Having experienced the disorder of the Roman civil wars, Virgil became a supporter of the empire and Emperor Augustus.

2. His works include two pastoral poems idealizing the simplicity of rural life, an appealing theme to urban Rome.

3. His epic poem, the *Aeneid,* was funded by Augustus. At the end of his life, Virgil had not finished his revisions; he ordered his manuscript burned at his death, but Augustus prevented its destruction.

4. Written in Latin, the *Aeneid* is intended to make Latin a poetic vehicle with a cultural status similar to Greek and to assert Augustus's ancestral link to Aeneas.

5. The first six books are modeled after the *Odyssey;* the rest are modeled on the *Iliad.*

6. The main focus is the historicizing of myth, linking its characters with individual events and persons in Roman history.

7. The narration includes the reign of Aeneas and his son, the conquest of Greece, the expansion of Rome, and the reign of Julius Caesar and Augustus.

8. The Punic Wars and the Carthaginian invasion of Rome are predicted in Dido's curse on Aeneas when he leaves her.

9. The first role of the city is to create good conditions for civilized life; to establish good government; to erect buildings and monuments; and to encourage arts, theater, trade, and commerce. If the city leader neglects these tasks, the city will suffer.

10. The second role of the city is to spread its civilization, even if it entails fighting wars.

11. While we may regard this as imperialist aggression, many lands welcomed the Roman security, technology, improved economy, and opportunities for Roman citizenship and for advancement in the Roman bureaucracy.

12. While the *Iliad* and the *Odyssey* focus on the heroes of the epics, Rome—not Aeneas—is the true subject of the *Aeneid.* In the *Iliad,* Zeus sympathized with both sides, but the *Aeneid* is seen from a Roman viewpoint: fighting for Rome is honorable, whereas fighting for personal glory, as Turnus did, is not.

13. The *Aeneid* expresses a nostalgia for the imagined simplicity of the past, a sign that the price paid for civilization may have been too high.

14. The Greek heroes received some kind of reward for their troubles; Aeneas will not even get to see the Rome for which he has sacrificed everything.

15. While Achilles and Odysseus had a choice of fates, Aeneas must do as the gods have predetermined: go to Italy when ordered by Venus and leave his lover, Dido, when ordered by Mercury.

16. The gods impose suffering on a good man for the good of Rome. Aeneas is aware of his burden, literally carrying the household gods of Troy—the Lares, Penates, and Vesta—to Rome.

17. Whereas Achilles was excessive and Odysseus impulsive, Aeneas exhibits self-control, responsibility, and compassion.

18. In book 10, Virgil contrasts the behavior of Turnus with that of Aeneas, a contrast between Greek and Roman heroic styles. Turnus kills Pallas (Aeneas's lover) and wears his belt to boast of his victory. Aeneas treats a young enemy, Lausus, with respect and refuses to strip the armor when the youth is killed.

19. When Aeneas's anger is roused, it is terrible, but it is caused by moral outrage, not slights to his ego.

20. The women in the *Aeneid* are divided into those for and those against Rome. Pro-Roman are Creusa, Aeneas's wife, and his mother, Venus.

21. Creusa, left behind at Troy, is killed by Greek soldiers; Aeneas returns and sees only her shade, an image of her insubstantial value. She instructs him to accept his fate and seek a new kingdom and wife.

22. Marriage is a sacred Roman institution, but one for which love is not essential. Aeneas weds the Latin Princess Lavinia for political reasons; Dido, whom he loves, he does not marry. Fatherhood is essential, while motherhood is subsumed in the larger affairs of state.

23. Thetis, Achilles's mother, is a messenger like Venus; while Thetis prefers a long life for her son, Venus has a political agenda for Aeneas, even if it means that he will suffer.

24. Juno and Juturna (Turnus's sister) are anti-Roman forces, interfering to prevent Aeneas's victory. Juno calls up the powers of Allecto, one of the Furies, from the Underworld.

25. Juno succeeds in delaying Aeneas but, in the process, kills those she supported.

26. Dido is portrayed sympathetically as a victim of the gods as well as of Aeneas. Abandoned by him, she kills herself. On a personal level, Virgil sympathizes with her, but he also sees her as having neglected her civic duties.

27. Venus removes the cloud from Aeneas's eyes so that he can see the destruction of Troy from the gods' viewpoint, but unlike the similar situation in the *Iliad* where Athene lets Diomedes see the gods on the battlefield, humans in the *Aeneid* are merely agents in a divine plan, and their actions are insignificant.

28. Human destiny is a function of divine politics, including the love between Dido and Aeneas. The only choice is how to respond to the burdens doled out by the gods.

29. In the Underworld, Aeneas learns the meaning of his suffering from the shade of his father, Anchises.

30. Using the *Odyssey* and Plato's *Phaedo*, Virgil describes the Underworld as divided into nine circles administering justice to human souls.

31. Where the highway divides, leading to Tartarus and Elysium, Anchises serves as Aeneas's moral guide and explains how the good are rewarded in eternity and how most souls are reincarnated in endless cycles, each getting what he or she deserves.

32. Anchises also explains the future of Rome; this brings Aeneas to accept his burden with a new commitment.

33. Some evidence suggests that the view of Rome triumphant is ironic; however, if that is the case, then Augustus as well as other readers have missed the irony for two millennia.

34. Despite the Roman preference for demythologizing, Aeneas must go to the Underworld as an obligatory voyage. The voyage is, however, presented by Virgil as an illusion, or possibly as a reminder that every dream may turn into a nightmare.

35. The climax of the *Aeneid,* the combat between Turnus and Aeneas, parallels the combat between Hector and Achilles; however, in the *Iliad* the outcome was not determined beforehand, whereas in the *Aeneid* the gods know the outcome in advance.

36. Achilles, in his rage, refuses to listen to pleas for Hector's body to be respected; Aeneas is willing to listen to similar pleas, until he sees the general wearing the belt of Pallas.

37. Some readers argue that this shows Aeneas as an agent of a corrupt, imperialist government, his humanity destroyed. From being a model Roman hero he has become a Greek hero. Others see the scene as representing a gap between the public figure and the private man.

38. Others argue that Aeneas starts out as a Greek-style hero but becomes a model Roman hero over time.

39. Differences between the *Iliad* and the *Aeneid* include the characters of Patrocles and Pallas; Patrocles was an experienced fighter, whereas Pallas was a youth, and Turnus's boast of the kill was unwarranted.

40. The *Aeneid*'s world consists of people who are suffering losses because they are burdened with the need to serve and are deceived by gods with political agendas. However, there is no alternative: war is recognized as the ultimate horror.

41. There is a conflict between humanism and war, and perhaps a conflict between humanism and government; but if war is too high a price to pay for civilization, then humans are condemned to live in a world where the forces of libido are in control.

PRIMARY TEXT SELECTION: Virgil, *Aeneid*

KEY NAMES OF MYTHOLOGICAL CHARACTERS MENTIONED

Aeneas, the sole surviving hero from Troy, son of Venus (Aphrodite)

Creusa, his wife, dead at Troy

Anchises, Aeneas's father

Turnus, the military leader of the Latins

Pallas, Aeneas's lover, killed by Turnus

Dido, the woman he loves

Mercury (Hermes)

Lavinia, Aeneas's Latin wife

King Latinus, her father

KEY NAMES ASSOCIATED WITH THE TELLING/CRITICISM OF MYTHS

Virgil (70–19 B.C.)

CHAPTER 22

OVID'S *METAMORPHOSES:*
THE RETELLING OF GREEK MYTHS

MAIN POINTS

1. Something in Ovid's writings offended Augustus, who banished him from Rome; perhaps he found that Ovid's cynical depictions of gods and humans undermined the official image of sober Roman citizens.

2. Ovid's theme in *Metamorphoses* is "bodies changed."

3. Narrative links allow one tale to grow into another, reflecting the theme of transformation in the structure of the poem itself.

4. Beginning with creation, Ovid's universe moves from chaos to order, where chaos is viewed as an intolerable condition; god, or nature, subdivides all creation and makes out boundaries, similar to the subdivisions of Rome.

5. Ovid is poking fun at Augustus, equating him with Jupiter, satirizing his attempt at imposing moral restraint on the elite patrician class.

6. Throughout much of the work, Ovid uses parody, mocking the gods and perhaps Augustus himself.

7. Behind the witty surface lurks a bitter indictment; his section on the Ages of Man includes Rome as an example of the Iron Age, characterized by greed and violence.

8. Romans were caught between the terror of anarchy and the threat of law; for Ovid, the role of the government in the Iron Age is to use force to impose order.

9. Many of Ovid's tales portray a world of vice, characterized by lust, rape, betrayal, and revenge, perhaps a comment on the cruelty of those in power. The only escape is to be transformed into something less than human: trees, rocks, or constellations.

10. "The Story of Perseus" shows the compulsion toward immobility: Perseus turns all of Andromeda's suitors to stone at once by showing them the Gorgon's head. Literally, this is a Roman petrification of Greek myth.

11. The gods' sensual desires remain unfulfilled, as their human objects turn to inanimate things, such as Daphne turning into a laurel tree while fleeing Apollo. The only escape for her is to be dehumanized.

12. The *Metamorphoses* ends with the deification of Caesar, a fairly serious section; however, Ovid implies in the "Epilogue" that his own fame will rise higher than Caesar's.

13. Even though Rome fell, Ovid remained one of the most important influences on Western culture.

KEY NAMES OF MYTHOLOGICAL CHARACTERS MENTIONED

Jupiter

Apollo

Lycaeon, an Arcadian tyrant turned into a sheep

Deucalion and Pyrrha, survivors of the Flood

Themis

Daphne, the nymph pursued by Apollo

Peneus, her father, a river god

Perseus

Andromeda, the Ethiopian princess he saves

The Gorgon, Medusa

KEY NAMES ASSOCIATED WITH THE TELLING/CRITICISM OF MYTHS

Ovid, Roman poet (43 B.C.–A.D. 17)

CHAPTER 23

THE PERSISTENCE OF MYTH

MAIN POINTS

1. Classical mythology has continued to provide a cultural resource, long after its connection to belief systems has ceased.

2. During the Dark Ages much knowledge and interest in classical learning was lost, and the hero of classical mythology was considered inappropriate for a Christian focus on humility and otherworldliness.

3. In the late Middle Ages classical mythology was rediscovered through the works of Virgil and Ovid and was made acceptable through a Christian reinterpretation.

4. Such reinterpretations include Virgil's prediction of the Coming of Christ and Dante's transformation of Virgil's description of the Underworld with borrowed elements from Greek mythology.

5. The Courtly Love tradition sparked a revived interest in Ovid's *Art of Love,* and it inspired Dante and Petrarch.

6. The popular uses of classical mythology in the modern world include mythic materials in psychology, sociology, television, and advertising.

7. Mythic material is most frequently transmitted in four basic ways: (1) making ancient plays or poems accessible to modern readers through modern translations and performances; (2) updating ancient stories to make them relevant to contemporary audiences; (3) borrowing familiar mythic themes and images to create a double vision, ancient and modern; (4) using a mythic figure as an emblem or a symbol.

8. The study of Greek was revived in the Renaissance after having been unpopular during the Middle Ages; English translators include George Chapman and Alexander Pope.

9. Revisionist versions of the classics existed even in classical Greece with Aeschylus, Sophocles, and Euripides. Ovid continued the revisionist tradition.

10. When classical drama was revived in the Renaissance, playwrights began revising classical plays. European playwrights such as Shakespeare, Racine, O'Neill, Gide, Giraudoux, Sartre, and Anouilh have revised classical drama.

11. Anouilh wrote a version of *Antigone* (1944) intended as a criticism of the Vichy government during World War II.

12. Opera may have its origin in a desire to revive Greek drama in its supposed original form of a singing stage performance.

13. Other opera composers incorporating Greek mythology in their works are Monteverdi, Purcell, Richard Strauss, and Stravinsky.

14. Writers of fiction using material from Greek mythology include Shakespeare, John Barth, James Joyce, and Derek Walcott.

15. Frequently, writers, artists, and composers have employed mythic images or mythic themes; names include Botticelli, Jean Cousin the Elder, Claude Lorrain, Lord Tennison, Yeats, Dali, Auden, and Picasso.

16. The following novels include extended uses of mythic themes: Updike's *The Centaur,* Joyce's *Portrait of the Artist as a Young Man,* and Malamud's *The Natural.*

17. In these cases, the mythic material provides a deeper understanding of the experiences of the human condition.

18. Some writers use specific mythic figures as a symbol of an idea, such as Freud's use of Oedipus, Camus's use of Sisyphus, ecologists' use of Gaea, and feminist psychologists' use of Athene, Artemis, and Aphrodite.

19. Myths can provide information about cultural changes, for example, through the study of revisions. The story of Orpheus and Eurydice has been interpreted as a grand but tragic passion, as a descent into the depths of the human psyche, and as a descent into existential despair. Artists revising the story include Monteverdi, Gluck, Haydn, Anouilh, Cocteau, Williams, Lumet, and Abdoh.

20. Two seventeenth-century painters, Rubens and Poussin, each portrayed the rape of the Sabine women, one a violent and the other a more detached version.

21. Dali comments ironically on Ingres's painting *The Apotheosis of Homer* in his own painting of the same name.

22. Interpretations of Venus throughout the centuries reveal much about these eras, with the images ranging from a calm depiction of divine beauty, an idealization, and a sensuous portrayal, to a modern parody.

23. A whole generation may latch on to a particular mythic figure as a cultural icon. Examples are Icarus and Prometheus.

24. The Renaissance included a revival of Greek classical mythology, and Christian humanists utilized classical mythic images without any sense of blasphemy.

25. For example, Sir Philip Sidney's sonnets deal with the conflict between Ovidian images and Christian belief, promoting a balance between the impulses of the heart and the journey of the soul to heaven.

26. During the Renaissance, biblical figures were portrayed as Greek gods while mythological stories were depicted in Renaissance costumes and settings.

27. For the Greeks, Icarus represented a lesson in the necessity of the Golden Mean of moderation; during the Renaissance, he became a symbol of the audacious spirit breaking through the limits of conventions and paying a high price.

28. Icarus becomes the mythic model for Doctor Faustus, the Renaissance man who, doomed to fail, must follow his ambition to exceed the pre-set limits.

29. The Baroque painter Breughel the Elder uses the figure of Icarus to signal a shift in cultural values from the human-centered world of the Renaissance to the asymmetrical Baroque perspective of a world in which the individual has no intrinsic significance.

30. In the Romantic period, Prometheus became the symbol of a generation of artists, composers, poets, and novelists such as Byron and Shelley.

31. Shelley compares Prometheus with Satan but sees him as the highest perfection of moral and intellectual nature in his rebellion against tyranny.

32. Napoleon was compared to Prometheus until he declared himself emperor; Beethoven removed the dedication to Napoleon from his Third Symphony for this reason.

33. The image of Satan-as-hero prompted a revival of interest in Milton and his *Paradise Lost,* and Shelley's wife, Mary Shelley, entitled her novel *Frankenstein, or the Modern Prometheus.*

34. During the Renaissance such pursuit was identified with Faustus, symbolized by Icarus; in the Romantic period the character of Faustus was revived by Goethe and others, but now symbolized by Prometheus.

NOTE: In the character of Doctor Faustus we witness the mythopoeic (myth-making) cultural force in modern times; the character was based on a scientist in Württemberg, Germany, in the sixteenth century, Johann Faust; Faust was an astrologer and an alchemist who had hopes of turning base metals into gold. Marlowe wrote his story of Faust some fifty years after Faust's death; since then, Faust himself has become a modern myth, an image of the person who is willing to give up everything most other people consider sacred for the sake of pure knowledge (or, in some cases, for profit) and who will pay dearly for this bargain. Although Faust himself was compared to Icarus in the Renaissance and Prometheus in the Romantic period, the mythologized figure of the doctor has emerged in modern times as an icon in its own right, used as a mythic theme in novels and films. Whereas Mary Shelley compared her Doctor Frankenstein to Prometheus, later film versions of the story tend explicitly or implicitly to compare Frankenstein to the single-minded, success-obsessed Doctor Faust instead.

---

35. Classical myths have retained their capacity to convey meaning to us, and will undoubtedly continue to express the continuity of the human spirit.

PRIMARY TEXT SELECTIONS: Dante, *The Inferno;* Sir Philip Sidney, Sonnet 5 from *Astrophel and Stella;* John Lyly, Song from *Alexander and Campaspe;* John Donne, "Love's Deity"; John Milton, *Paradise Lost;* George Gordon, Lord Byron, *Prometheus;* Alfred, Lord Tennyson, "Ulysses"; William Butler Yeats, "Leda and the Swan"; W. H. Auden, "The Shield of Achilles" and "Musée des Beaux Arts."

KEY NAMES OF MYTHOLOGICAL CHARACTERS MENTIONED

Narcissus

Oedipus

Sisyphus

Gaea

Athene

Artemis

Aphrodite

Orpheus

Eurydice

Icarus

Prometheus

Doctor Faustus, semi-historical character; sold his soul to the devil for knowledge

KEY NAMES ASSOCIATED WITH THE TELLING/CRITICISM OF MYTHS

Virgil (70–19 B.C.)

Ovid (43 B.C.–17 A.D.)

Dante Alighieri, Italian poet (1265–1321)

Petrarch, Italian scholar and poet (1304–1374)

George Chapman, English translator of Homer (1557–1643)

Alexander Pope, English poet (1688–1744)

Aeschylus (c. 525–456 B.C.)

Sophocles (c. 495–406 B.C.)

Euripides (c. 485–406 B.C.)

Seneca, Roman dramatist (c. 3 B.C.–65 A.D.)

William Shakespeare, English dramatist (1564–1616)

Jean Racine, French dramatist (1639–1699)

Eugene O'Neill, English dramatist (1888–1953)

Andre Gide, French novelist (1869–1951)

Jean Giraudoux, French novelist (1882–1944)

Jean-Paul Sartre, French philosopher and dramatist (1905–1980)

Jean Anouilh, French dramatist (1910–1987)

Claudio Monteverdi, Italian composer (1567–1643)

Henry Purcell, English composer (c. 1658–1695)

Richard Strauss, German composer (1864–1949)

Igor Stravinsky, Russian composer (1882–1971)

James Joyce, Irish novelist (1882–1941)

Sandro Botticelli, Italian painter (c. 1445–1510)

Jean Cousin the Elder (died c. 1560)

Claude Gellée, called Lorrain, French painter (1600–1682)

Alfred, Lord Tennyson, English poet (1809–1892)

William Butler Yeats, Irish poet (1865–1939)

Salvador Dali, Spanish painter (1904–1989)

W. H. Auden, American poet (1907–1973)

Pablo Picasso, Spanish painter (1881–1973)

John Updike, American writer (1932–)

Bernard Malamud, American writer (1914–1986)

Sigmund Freud, Austrian psychoanalyst (1856–1939)

Albert Camus, French philosopher and novelist (1913–1960)

Christoph Willibald Gluck, German composer (1714–1787)

Franz Joseph Haydn, German composer (1732–1809)

Jean Cocteau, French dramatist and film director (1891–1963)

Sidney Lumet, American film director (1924–)

Tennessee Williams, American dramatist (1914–1983)

Peter Paul Rubens, Flemish painter (1577–1640)

Nicolas Poussin, French painter (c. 1593–1665)

Jean-Auguste-Dominique Ingres, French painter (1780–1867)

Tiziano Vecellio, called Titian, Italian painter (c. 1490–1576)

Sir Philip Sidney, English poet (1554–1586)

Christopher Marlowe, English dramatist (1564–1593)

Pieter Breughel the Elder, Dutch painter (1525–1569)

George Gordon, Lord Byron, English poet (1788–1824)

Percy Bysshe Shelley, English poet (1792–1822)

Mary Wollstonecraft Shelley, English novelist (1797–1851)

John Milton, English poet (1608–1674)

Johann Wolfgang von Goethe, German scholar, poet and novelist (1749–1832)

Eugene Delacroix, French painter (1798–1863)

Charles-François Gounod, French composer (1818–1893)

Hector Berlioz, French composer (1803–1869)

PART II
TEST QUESTIONS

CHAPTER 1
INTRODUCTION TO THE NATURE OF MYTH

TRUE/FALSE QUESTIONS

1. The goddess Athene burst from Zeus's thigh, wearing a warrior's spear and shield. (F)

2. The birth of Athene illustrates a mythical paradox: a male creating new life without the participation of a mother. (T)

3. In Greek myth, supernatural beings are almost always present. (T)

4. Like dreams, myths are fundamentally without relation to external reality. (F)

5. All mythic events are grounded in the values, attitudes, and expectations of the society producing the myths. (T)

6. The word *myth* literally means "false speech." (F)

7. Scholars recognize that myth may have a truth of its own that transcends mere fact. (T)

8. The earliest literary work based on myth is the Sumerian story of Gilgamesh. (T)

9. Greek and Mesopotamian mythmakers share a belief in a vertically structured, three-story universe: heaven, earth, and the Underworld. (T)

10. Greek and Mesopotamian mythmakers share a belief that the human soul can, with good behavior, expect to share an afterlife in heaven with the gods. (F)

11. Apollodorus of Athens is believed by most scholars to be the true author of the *Library*. (F)

12. Virgil, the author of the *Metamorphoses of the Gods*, is generally thought to be a staunch supporter of Roman imperialism. (F)

13. The *Metamorphoses of the Gods* was written by the Roman poet Ovid during the reign of Augustus. (T)

14. The archaeologist Heinrich Schliemann excavated the traditional site of Mount Olympus. (F)

15. The Mycenaean civilization was strongly influenced by an even older civilization, the Minoan civilization. (T)

16. The Greek myth of Theseus goes back to Minoan times, featuring the story of the Minotaur. (T)

17. It is possible for literary works of myth to contain elements of folklore. (T)

18. The Greek poets reinterpreted Greek mythology with an orientation towards humanistic values. (T)

19. There is a basic similarity between the artistic representation of deities by Egyptian artists, and by Greek artists: Both endeavor to create images of gods resembling humans not only physically but also psychologically. (F)

20. Greek myth typically emphasizes competitiveness and individual achievement. (T)

MULTIPLE-CHOICE QUESTIONS

21. The images of Athene and Dionysus suggest
    a. that myth has power to integrate polar opposites, illustrating contrareties and conflicts inherent in existence. (*)
    b. that knowledge of procreation and genetics was beyond the scope of Greek mythology.
    c. that myth has the capacity to illustrate problematic relationships in dysfunctional families.
    d. that myth, essentially, makes very little sense.

22. The word *myth* (Greek: *mythos*) literally means
    a. "false speech."
    h "utterance." (*)
    c. "ancient story."
    d. "divine law."

23. The Sumerian *Epic of Gilgamesh* contains, among other themes, a version of a familiar mythic theme. Which one is it?
    a. the theme of virgin birth
    b. the theme of sacred, powerful twins
    c. the theme of the divine sacrifice of the hero
    d. the theme of a global flood   (*)

24. The Greek philosopher Aristotle defines myth as
    a. a Homeric hymn.
    b. a plot structure in a literary work. (*)
    c. a tall tale.
    d. a tragic drama.

25. Three key names are associated with the preservation of Greek mythology in the first centuries B.C. and A.D. Choose the one that doesn't belong on the list.
    a. Apollodorus of Athens
    b. Pausanias
    c. Plutarch
    d. Virgil (*)

26. According to some scholars, there is a difference between the terms *legendary* and *mythic*. What is the difference?
    a. *Legendary* means that the story has some nucleus of historical truth, and *mythic* means fictional. (*)
    b. *Legendary* means fictional, and *mythic* means that the story has some nucleus of historical truth.
    c. *Legendary* means we can discern what historical truth is, and *mythic* means that we can never know if the story is historically true.
    d. Trick question. There is no difference between *legendary* and *mythic,* according to most scholars.

27. Scholars agree that most Greek myths originated
    a. between about 1600 and 1100 B.C. (*)
    b. between about 700 and 500 B.C.
    c. between about 140 B.C. and 160 A.D.
    d. at least 10,000 years ago.

28. Who was the Minotaur?
    a. a monster which was half-human and half-dolphin
    b. a monster which was half-human and half-bull (*)
    c. the king of Knossos, Crete.
    d. a centaur, half-human and half-horse

29. What kind of stories do typical sagas deal with?
    a. stories about a particular city or family (*)
    b. stories about the origin of the world
    c. stories about the experiences of the common folk
    d. stories about gods in disguise interacting with heroes

30. A certain Greek hero is mentioned as demonstrating the typical Greek emphasis on individualism. Who is he?
    a. Herodotus
    b. Achilles (*)
    c. Theseus
    d. Virgil

ESSAY QUESTIONS

31. Define the concept of individualism, using an example from Greek mythology.

32. Describe the difference between sagas and folktales.

33. How can Greek myth be said to emphasize humanism?

CHAPTER 2
WAYS OF INTERPRETING MYTH

TRUE/FALSE QUESTIONS

1. In contrast to depicting scenes of violent conflict on Mount Olympus, the Parthenon frieze depicts the scenes of human life as calm and serene. (F)

2. Apollo's twin sister was Artemis, the goddess of wildlife and the hunt. (T)

3. The Homeric hymns should be regarded as the ancient Greek equivalent of the Judeo-Christian Bible and the Islamic Qur'an in terms of having binding authority of scripture. (F)

4. The Greek philosophical movement changed the way Greek writers viewed their mythology virtually overnight, plunging Greece into an age of general skepticism. (F)

5. Euripides interprets the myth of the birth of Dionysus as an allegory. (T)

6. In one allegorical interpretation, the Greek gods become symbols of natural phenomena and human dispositions. (T)

7. Anaxagoras interpreted Greek myths as allegories of morals and virtue. (T)

8. Xenophanes of Colophon objected to the lack of virtue among the gods. (T)

9. Euhemerus of Messene founded the theory of Euhemerism, stating that there is no factual basis for myth; it is all a matter of psychological tensions in the human mind. (F)

10. Euhemerism is the term for the theory, expressed by Euhemerus of Messene, that the Greek gods were originally mortal kings who had been deified posthumously. (T)

11. One of the two general meanings of the term *mythology* is the methodological study of myths, particularly in terms of their form, purpose, and function. (T)

12. The nature myth theory was advocated by Carl Jung. (F)

13. The theory of ritual is an externalist theory of myth. (T)

14. The charter theory claims that myths validate existing customs, beliefs, and practices. (T)

15. Freudian theory claims that "dream-work" condenses and rearranges ordinary events of daily life into images that express and conceal subconscious desire. (T)

16. The story of King Oedipus is used to illustrates the Freudian theory of male infantile sexuality. (T)

17. Freud divides the mind into three basic components: the *id,* the *ego,* and the *collective unconscious.* (F)

18. Carl Jung postulates that within the mind of every man exists a male image, the animus, and within every female exists a female soul, the anima. (F)

19. According to Joseph Campbell, the hero's rites of passage represent stages in the hero's psychological development and maturation. (T)

20. Structuralism claims that myths reflect the tripartite structure of the psyche, dividing every story into three components: the Underworld, the earth, and the realm of the gods. (F)

MULTIPLE-CHOICE QUESTIONS

21. Who was Apollo's twin sister?
    a. Athene
    b. Artemis (*)
    c. the queen of the Amazon warriors
    d. Demeter

22. What is Euhemerism?
    a. the theory, expressed by Euhemerus of Messene, that the Greek gods were originally paragons of virtue, but later generations of poets misrepresented their moral qualities
    b. the theory, expressed by Euhemerus of Messene, that the Greek myths should be viewed as the ultimate moral authority and social blueprint
    c. the theory, expressed by Euhemerus of Athens, that myths are, basically, lies told by the priesthood in order to subdue the population
    d. the theory, expressed by Euhemerus of Messene, that the Greek gods were originally mortal kings who had been deified posthumously (*)

23. One of the two general meanings of the word *mythology* is a set or a system of myths. Which is the other?
    a. a psychological, pathological tendency to make up lies
    b. the scientific study of artifacts belonging to the culture of the myth
    c. the methodological study of myths, particularly in terms of their form, purpose, and function (*)
    d. the psychological study of a person's self-image through the stories (myths) one tells about oneself

24. A theory of myth claims that myths are narratives which supply the rationale for some ritual or custom in order to help maintain social stability. Identify the name of the theory and its chief proponent.
    a. the ritual theory; Sir James Frazer
    b. the charter theory; Bronislaw Malinowski (*)
    c. the nature myth theory; F. Max Müller
    d. the structuralist theory; Claude Lévi-Strauss

25. Identify the criticism of the theory of ritual:
    a. It does not explain why rituals develop in the first place. (*)
    b. It fails to explain why human welfare is favored over divine prerogative.
    c. It does not explain the similarity between myths and dreams.
    d. Not all myths present a quantitative division of opposites.

26. Why did Zeus accept as the gods' share of the sacrifice an inedible pile of bones covered with fat, according to Hesiod?
    a. He wanted humans to have the more nutritious part of the animal.
    b. He drew lots with the Titan Prometheus, and Prometheus won.
    c. He was tricked by Prometheus to choose the better-looking pile. (*)
    d. The gods crave bones, contrary to humans.

27. Who was Pandora?
    a. the mother of Zeus
    b. the first woman (*)
    c. King Oedipus's mother and wife
    d. the goddess of small containers and enclosures

28. Freudian theory uses the story of King Oedipus to illustrate mythic wish fulfillment. Which component of the psyche is illuminated by Oedipus's destiny of killing his father and marrying his mother?
    a. the superego
    b. the ego
    c. the collective unconscious
    d. the id (*)

29. Jungian theory operates with the concept of "the anima." What is the anima?
    a. the animal drives of human beings which must be controlled
    b. the immortal soul which inhabits the body while we are alive and leaves the body when we die
    c. the female side of a man's psyche (*)
    d. the female side of a woman's psyche

30. What is the approach of structuralism to myths?
    a. Myths are believed to reflect the tripartite structure of the psyche, thus dividing every story into three components: the Underworld, the earth, and the realm of the gods.
    b. Myth is believed to be primitive science, attempting to explain natural phenomena.
    c. Myths, like dreams, contain universal archetypes springing from the collective unconscious.
    d. Myth is viewed as a reflection of the mind's binary organization: humans project a binary significance onto experience, dividing everything into polar opposites. (*)

ESSAY QUESTIONS

31. Describe the charter theory of myth, using an example.

32. Describe Freud's theory of the tripartite psyche, and relate it to the story of King Oedipus.

33. Define the concept of "the anima," and explain its function in Jungian theory.

CHAPTER 3

IN THE BEGINNING: HESIOD'S *THEOGONY*

TRUE/FALSE QUESTIONS

1. The Greek mythic model of the cosmos was created in close collaboration with Greek scientists of the era. (F)

2. The term *cosmogony* means a theory of the creation or origin of the universe. (T)

3. One of the nine muses of the arts is the muse of astronomy. (T)

4. According to some scholars, Hesiod's *Theogony* contains much autobiographical material. (T)

5. One of the themes shared by the Greek cosmogony and its Near Eastern antecedents is the theme of the slaying of the monster snake. (T)

6. Zeus is the grandson of Gaea and Cronus. (F)

7. Zeus castrates his father, Cronus, and throws his genitals into the sea. (F)

8. Aphrodite rises out of the sea, born of the severed phallus, semen, and sea foam. (T)

9. In order to avoid Cronus's fate, Uranus devours his children. (F)

10. Some scholars speculate that the castration myth reflects an ancient ritual in which the primal goddess's consort was killed and perhaps eaten. (T)

11. Some scholars speculate that Zeus's swallowing Metis and subsequently giving birth to Athene reflects an ancient custom of cannibalism within the tribe or family. (F)

12. As a charter myth, the birth of Athene validates the institution of cannibalism. (F)

13. As an etiological myth, the birth of Athene signifies a shift from matriarchal to patriarchal rule. (T)

14. A structuralist interpretation of the birth of Athene sees the story as a reconciliation of the natural, instinctual component of humans, represented by Metis, and the rational intellect, represented by Zeus. (F)

15. Hera may have been worshiped as a goddess in her own right before patriarchal religion reduced her to the status of Zeus's consort. (T)

16. Hera gives birth to the monster Hephaestus, who defeats Zeus in a great battle. (F)

17. Hephaestus is the only disabled god on Mount Olympus. (T)

18. Gaea makes Zeus confront her own child, the monster Hephaestus. (F)

19. The battle between Zeus and the monster snake may be a faint memory of some geological disaster. (T)

20. Hesiod is generally pessimistic about the human social and moral values. (T)

MULTIPLE-CHOICE QUESTIONS

21. There are several themes mentioned in the text which are shared by the cosmogony of Hesiod and the Near Eastern myths. Which of the following is not one of those themes?
    a. Several generations of gods successively rule the cosmos before the young male sky god takes over.
    b. A snakelike monster is slain by the young male god.
    c. The older god is castrated by a younger god.
    d. The older generation of gods perishes in a global flood. (*)

22. Why is Uranus castrated?
    a. Gaea is resentful toward him for not letting her give birth to her children. (*)
    b. Gaea is resentful toward him for having had sexual relationships with other female deities.
    c. Gaea is resentful toward him for having had sexual relationships with mortal women.
    d. Tartarus is appalled because Uranus has married his own mother.

23. Who devoured his children?
    a. Typhoeus
    b. Cronus (*)
    c. Zeus
    d. Uranus

24. There are nine Muses. Which one of these four is not a Muse?
    a. Clio
    b. Urania
    c. Rhea (*)
    d. Thalia

25. What is the charter function of the myth of Athene's birth?
    a. It validates the institution of cannibalism.
    b. It validates patriarchy and the institution of marriage in which the husband has total control of the wife. (*)
    c. It validates matriarchy and the institution of the ritual slaying of the goddess's consort.
    d. There is no charter function of this particular myth.

26. What is the name of the monster snake slain by Zeus?
     a. Typhoeus (*)
     b. Hephaestus
     c. Tiamat
     d. Tartarus

27. Who is the mother of the Muses?
     a. Mnemosyne (*)
     b. Clio
     c. Hera
     d. Athene

28. Who is quoted as saying the following? "Listen, you country bumpkins, you swag-bellied yahoos, / we know how to tell many lies that pass for truth, . . ."
     a. Hesiod, speaking to his readers
     b. Athene, speaking to the city of Athens
     c. the Muses, speaking to Hesiod (*)
     d. the Furies, speaking to mortal men and women

29. In the *Theogony*, Hesiod tells of Prometheus tricking Zeus. Identify the situation.
     a. He is tricking Zeus into having an incestuous relationship with his own mother.
     b. He is tricking Zeus into accepting animal bones as a sacrifice. (*)
     c. He is tricking Zeus into fighting with the monster snake.
     d. He is tricking Zeus into creating the first woman.

30. In a passage in the *Theogony,* a god is creating the first woman at the request of Zeus. His name is not mentioned, but can you identify him from this description? "The famous lame smith took clay and, through Zeus's counsels, gave it the shape of a modest maiden."
     a. Apollo
     b. Hephaestus (*)
     c. Hermes
     d. Prometheus

ESSAY QUESTIONS

31. Define *cosmology* and *cosmogony*.

32. Discuss the paradox involved in the birth of Aphrodite from an act of sexual mutilation.

33. Explain the following passage from the *Theogony* in terms of the mythological characters involved, and relate it to one or more theories of myth:

> But majestic Kronos kept on swallowing each child
> as it moved from the holy womb towards the knees;
> his purpose was to prevent any other child of the Sky Dwellers
> from holding the kingly office among immortals.
> He had learned from Gaia and starry Ouranos
> that he, despite his power, was fated
> to be subdued by his own son, a victim of his own schemes.

CHAPTER 4

THE WORLD IN DECLINE:
ALIENATION OF THE HUMAN AND DIVINE

TRUE/FALSE QUESTIONS

1. Hesiod sees the rise of Zeus as beneficial to humans as well as to gods. (F)

2. Prometheus is chained to a rock by Zeus as punishment for tricking Zeus to accept bones of sacrificial animals. (F)

3. Pandora, the first woman, is created to punish man. (T)

4. There is a mythological connection between the appearance of Pandora and using fire for cooking. (T)

5. The Greek and Judeo-Christian traditions agree on seeing woman as the catalyst of humanity's historical decline. (T)

6. In Genesis, a serpent persuades Eve to eat from the Tree of Life. (F)

7. The forbidden fruit is the biblical counterpart of the Promethean fire: enlightenment and cultural separation from nature. (T)

8. When Pandora catches Hope before it flies out of the jar, she closes the lid, thus sealing off hope from the human heart forever. (F)

9. Enkidu, the savage male, is tamed through a sexual encounter with a priestess. (T)

10. Gilgamesh, the savage male, is tamed by a sexual encounter with Enkidu, a priest of Ishtar. (F)

11. Hesiod saw cosmos permeated with two forms of Strife: mindless aggression and healthy competition. (T)

12. Hesiod mentions four ages of history, corresponding to the four main metals. (F)

13. Among the ages of history mentioned by Hesiod are the Age of Iron and the Age of Copper. (F)

14. During the Age of Gold, men were immortal in both body and soul. (F)

15. During the Age of Silver, men's childhood lasted a hundred years. (T)

16. The Age of Heroes is one of the ages of history mentioned by Hesiod, even though it has no corresponding metal. (T)

17. One of the signs that the end of the world is near is that newborns will have gray hair. (T)

18. Hesiod's view of history is apocalyptic. (T)

19. One of the key elements in Hesiod's *Works and Days* is the story of the global flood, which Deucalion and Pyrrha survive in an ark. (F)

20. Deucalion and Pyrrha survive the flood in an ark, according to Greek tradition, and repopulate the earth by throwing stones over their shoulders. (T)

MULTIPLE-CHOICE QUESTIONS

21. Why was Prometheus chained to a mountain, with an eagle eating from his liver?
    a. as punishment for tricking Zeus to accept bones from sacrificial animals
    b. as punishment for creating the first woman, thus letting evil loose in the world
    c. as punishment for stealing fire from the gods and giving it to men (*)
    d. for no good reason: the story shows that the wrath of Zeus is illogical.

22. Why did Zeus ask Hephaestus to create Pandora?
    a. to punish men for conspiring with Prometheus (*)
    b. to punish women for being a threat to male security
    c. to reward men for turning over Prometheus to him for punishment
    d. to punish men for believing themselves to be gods

23. In the Bible as well as in Greek mythology, humanity pays a price for knowledge in terms of losing something precious. Which loss shouldn't be on the list?
    a. a loss of innocence
    b. a loss of paradise
    c. a loss of eternal life (*)
    d. a loss of peace

24. Hesiod mentions five ages of history. Which of the following is one of these ages?
    a. Trick question: Hesiod mentions four ages of history, not five.
    b. the Age of Mercury
    c. the Age of Iron (*)
    d. the Age of Copper

25. Zeus tells Prometheus, "The price for the stolen fire will be a gift of evil to charm the hearts of all men as they hug their own doom." What is he referring to?
    a. the chaining of Prometheus to the rock
    b. the creation of Pandora (*)
    c. the creation of the Tree of Life
    d. the creation of Eve

26. The races of mortals made of ash trees belong to which age?
   a. the Age of Heroes
   b. the Age of Bronze (*)
   c. the Age of Copper
   d. the Age of Iron

27. Hesiod's account of the ages of history can be interpreted in several ways. How might a Jungian theorist read the story?
   a. The ages of history can be read symbolically as archetypal images of the development of a human being, from the time of childhood to a gradual fall into maturity. (*)
   b. The ages of history can be seen to validate the political notion that classes form a permanent social hierarchy.
   c. The ages of history can be seen as an explanation of the inevitable changes of the seasons.
   d. The ages of history explain the origin of the iron hardness of the human heart.

ESSAY QUESTIONS

28. How does Pandora resemble Eve in the Book of Genesis? Are there any differences between Pandora and Eve?

29. Discuss the mythic themes of a lost Golden Age and the fall from grace. Can a Freudian or a Jungian approach help explain these themes?

31. Explain the following passage from *Works and Days,* and relate it to one or more theories of myth:

> Earlier, human tribes lived on this earth
> without suffering and toilsome hardship
> and without painful illnesses that bring death to men—
> a wretched life ages men before their time—
> but the woman with her hands removed the great lid of the jar
> and scattered its contents, bringing grief and cares to men.
> Only Hope stayed under the rim of the jar

CHAPTER 5
THE OLYMPIAN FAMILY OF ZEUS

TRUE/FALSE QUESTIONS

1. According to Herodotus, the Greeks have known their gods at least as long as the Egyptians have known theirs. (F)

2. Homer claims that Zeus and his two brothers, Hades and Poseidon, divided the world after a contest of strength. (F)

3. It is unclear whether Zeus is in control of Fate or Fate is superior to the gods. (T)

4. The Moirae are the same as the Fates. (T)

5. Hades rules the Underworld with his wife Eileithyia. (F)

6. Poseidon is the god of earthquakes as well as the god of the sea. (T)

7. Hephaestus's symbol is the tripod, indicative of his lowly work among the gods. (F)

8. Poseidon's symbol is the tripod, an instrument for creating enormous waves. (F)

9. Demeter is known as Ceres in the Roman tradition. (T)

10. Poseidon's Roman equivalent is Pluto. (F)

11. One of Persephone's functions is to represent the cycle of growth, death, and rebirth. (T)

12. When Persephone eloped with Hades, Demeter grieved so hard that the plants withered and died. (F)

13. Athene, the patron of wisdom and military victory, is, despite her female nature, a patron of male crafts such as carpentry. (F)

14. Apollo is protector of the Delphic Oracle. (T)

15. Hermes's son Asclepius counteracts the diseases brought by his uncle Apollo by bringing healing. (F)

16. Artemis is both the patron of the hunt and the protector of wild animals. (T)

17. According to Homer, Eros is the lover of Aphrodite. (F)

18. The Romans associated Ares with their local god Mars. (T)

19. Dionysus is the patron of the tragic drama. (T)

20. According to Homer, if a horse or a lion had gods, they would look like horses and lions. (F)

MULTIPLE-CHOICE QUESTIONS

21. Who is Cronus's Roman equivalent?
    a. Neptune
    b. Jove
    c. Vulcan
    d. Saturn (*)

22. Who is Poseidon's Roman equivalent?
    a. Neptune (*)
    b. Vulcan
    c. Pluto
    d. Saturn

23. Who is the Roman equivalent of Artemis?
    a. Minerva
    b. Diana (*)
    c. Vesta
    d. Venus

24. What was the later consequence of Athene's beauty contest with Hera and Aphrodite?
    a. the birth of Hephaestus
    b. the marriage of Aphrodite to Hephaestus
    c. the Trojan War (*)
    d. the Persian War

25. Hermes is the patron of different trades. Which one shouldn't be on the list?
    a. merchants
    b. thieves
    c. gamblers
    d. sailors (*)

26. Dionysus is the only Olympian god who is
    a. disabled.
    b. born human. (*)
    c. half man, half animal.
    d. ugly.

27. What was Xenophanes's religion?
    a. He was a skeptic, having no religion.
    b. He believed in the Olympic gods.
    c. He believed in the main religion of Asia Minor, the Great Goddess of the earth's fertility.
    d. He believed in an unknown god behind the manifestations of other gods. (*)

28. Identify the Greek tradition of assuming that the gods were once heroes who were deified by later generations:
    a. Homerism
    b. etiological theory
    c. Euhemerism (*)
    d. Euripidism

ESSAY QUESTIONS

29. Choose two to four Greek gods and explain their attributes and function in terms of nature myth theory.

30. Choose two to four Greek gods and explain their attributes and function in terms of a psychological theory.

31. Comment on the skeptical idea that "if a horse or a lion had gods, they would look like horses and lions," and identify the author.

CHAPTER 6

THE GREAT GODDESS AND THE GODDESSES:
THE DIVINE WOMAN IN GREEK MYTHOLOGY

TRUE/FALSE QUESTIONS

1. The triple nature of the Great Goddess is often portrayed as the figures of the maiden, the mother, and the mother-in-law. (F)

2. The serpent is associated with the Goddess because of its associations with the underworld as well as its ability to shed its skin. (T)

3. A common Goddess symbol in the Near East is the sun. (F)

4. The division of the Goddess into three functions may be a result of the invasion of Europe by a patriarchal culture worshiping sky gods. (T)

5. There is evidence that the snake has become associated with evil because it used to represent the power of evil in the Goddess religion. (F)

6. The hero of the patriarchal culture seeks individual achievement rather than a reconciliation and continuity between generations. (T)

7. The hero of the patriarchal culture is, in his contempt for women, frequently sexually oriented toward his own gender. (F)

8. Under the rule of patriarchy, the attributes of the Great Goddess were often interpreted as negative. (T)

9. *Sparagmos* is a term for the sacred marriage between the Goddess and her consort. (F)

10. Zeus's battle with the dragon Typhoeus is a version of the battle with the World Serpent incorporating the female archetype. (T)

11. Hecate represents the death-wielding aspect of the Great Goddess. (T)

12. The story of Persephone is often interpreted as a nature myth, symbolizing the planting and sprouting of the seed. (T)

13. The story of Persephone is frequently interpreted through a Euhemeristic approach: Once there was a young woman who was raped and killed; later generations created the story of the mother and daughter goddesses. (F)

14. Contrary to most ancient rituals, the rituals of the Eleusinian Mysteries are well known through extensive contemporary accounts. (F)

15. The *hieros gamos* was the ritual dismemberment of the male god or consort. (F)

16. The Thesmophoria was a sowing ritual, practiced by women initiates only. (T)

17. The myth of Persephone presents marriage as legal rape. (T)

18. Artemis inherits the chthonic aspect of the goddess, being associated with the moon and Hecate. (T)

19. Aphrodite's relationship with Eros signifies her dual role as goddess of love and war. (F)

20. The story of Demophon serves as a charter myth for the Eleusinian Mysteries. (T)

MULTIPLE-CHOICE QUESTIONS

21. There is evidence of Goddess worship in the ancient world
    a. from the Paleolithic through the Bronze Age. (*)
    b. from the Neolithic through the Iron Age.
    c. from the Neolithic through the Bronze Age.
    d. from the Paleolithic until the thirteenth century A.D.

22. The Great Goddess is associated with several animal symbols; which one is not among them?
    a. the serpent
    b. the cow
    c. the bird
    d. the horse (*)

23. Identify the correct term for the Goddess creating offspring without male assistance:
    a. hieros gamos
    b. matriarchy
    c. parthenogenesis (*)
    d. parasynapsis

24. Identify the meaning of *sparagmos*:
    a. the sacred marriage between the Goddess and her consort
    b. the ritual dismemberment and eating of the male god or consort (*)
    c. the sacred drink of the priestess of Demeter at Eleusis, a strong grain-based drink.
    d. the ritual seclusion of a young woman during her first menstruation

25. What is a "hieros gamos"?
    a. the ritual dismemberment and eating of the male god or consort
    b. the sacred marriage between the Goddess and her consort (*)
    c. the Goddess's ability to create offspring without male assistance
    d. a hero of the Olympic Games

26. Choose an example of how the Goddess's attributes may be transformed into a negative image as a result of the rule of patriarchy:
    a. the sacred bird is transformed to the Phoenix igniting itself
    b. the sacred snake is transformed to an evil dragon or a monster (*)
    c. the Goddess is transformed into having a death-wielding aspect
    d. the sacred cow is transformed into a belligerent goat or a ram

27. The maiden and mother aspects of the Great Goddess are separated and made subordinate to Zeus in the characters of three of the following goddesses; which one would not be on the list?
    a. Aphrodite
    b. Hera
    c. Athene
    d. Hecate (*)

28. Demeter has all the functions of the Great Goddess except
    a. parthenogenesis. (*)
    b. parasynapsis.
    c. the invention of agriculture.
    d. the function of a maiden.

29. As an etiological myth, the story of Persephone explains
    a. fatherhood and fatherly love.
    b. why there are seasons. (*)
    c. the practice of setting a place at the table for Demeter.
    d. why Hades is a rapist.

30. The *Homeric Hymn to Demeter* probably dates from
    a. the seventh century B.C. (*)
    b. the second century B.C.
    c. 43 A.D.
    d. the fourteenth century B.C.

ESSAY QUESTIONS

31. Explain how the Great Goddess can simultaneously incorporate the functions of being the source of life, of death, and of rebirth, and give examples of how these functions are divided among various goddesses in Greek myth.

32. Explain the transition from Goddess worship to the patriarchal religion of the sky gods: How did it happen, and what were the consequences for Greek myth?

33. What is a patriarchal culture?

34. Explain the following passage, and relate it to one or more theories of myth:

> Persephone, the exceedingly beautiful, gave her [Demeter] this response: "I
> will tell you, Mother, everything accurately. When the swift slayer of
> Argos came to me from Father Zeus and the others in heaven with the
> message to come out of Erebos, so that seeing me with your eyes you
> might cease from your anger and terrible wrath, I leapt up for joy. But he
> secretly insinuated a pomegranate seed, honey-sweet food, and though I
> was unwilling, he compelled me by force to taste it. . . ." Zeus the loud-
> crashing, the wide-voiced one, sent fair-haired Rhea as a messenger to
> them, to bring dark-gowned Demeter among the race of the gods: he
> promised to give her whatever honors she might choose among the
> immortal gods. He granted that her daughter should spend the third portion
> of the year in its cycle down in the misty darkness, but the other two with
> her mother and the other immortals.

CHAPTER 7

IN TOUCH WITH THE GODS: APOLLO'S ORACLE AT DELPHI

TRUE/FALSE QUESTIONS

1. The facade of the temple at Delphi was inscribed with the maxim "Love your Neighbor." (F)

2. Delphi was believed to be the location of the center of the earth's surface. (T)

3. Archaeologists have recently been able to verify the existence in the past of a cleft in the rocks at Delphi emitting toxic vapors. (F)

4. The origin of the Apollo worship at Delphi lies in the Olympic battle between male and female powers. (T)

5. Hera gave parthenogenic birth to the serpent Python. (F)

6. Apollo and his sister Artemis were born to Leto seeking refuge from Hera's wrath in a cave on Mount Parnassus, later to become the Oracle at Delphi. (F)

7. Only three years old, Apollo kills a bear. (F)

8. In some versions, Apollo kills the monster Typhoeus, while other versions have him kill the monster Python. (F)

9. After killing the dragon, Apollo exiles himself to atone for his guilt. (T)

10. Delphi represents a new order where guilt can be atoned, rather than paid for in blood. (T)

11. Every three years the slaying of the monster was reenacted at the Pythian Games. (F)

12. Every eight years Apollo's slaying of Python was reenacted in a religious drama, the Stepterion, by priests at Delphi. (T)

13. The priestess Pythia would sit on a trident in an underground chamber, inhale vapors from below, and utter prophecies in Greek verse. (F)

14. The Oracle lied when it told King Croesus that if he crossed the Persian border, a great nation would fall. (F)

15. Sophocles uses the myth of Oedipus to confirm that no one can escape fulfilling Delphi's prophecies. (T)

16. The youth Cyparissus loved his pet stag so much, that when he accidentally killed it, Apollo granted his wish to be transformed into a stag. (F)

17. The princess Coronis carried a mortal man's child when she fell in love with Apollo; that child became the first physician, Asclepius. (F)

18. When Asclepius learned to revive the dead, Zeus killed him with a thunderbolt. (T)

19. The cult of Asclepius used the symbol of the omphalos, two snakes entwining a winged rod, as the symbol of healing. (F)

20. The caduceus is Asclepius's symbol of healing. (T)

MULTIPLE-CHOICE QUESTIONS

21. What is an *omphalos*?
    a. a column raised in the honor of Apollo at the Pythian Games
    b. the navel of the world, displayed in Delphi as a piece of rock (*)
    c. Aesclepius's symbol of healing: two snakes entwining a rod
    d. the sound of Zeus's thunderbolt

22. What did Themistocles interpret the Delphic Oracle to mean when it advised the Greeks to defend Greece with a wooden wall?
    a. that they must build a wall around Athens
    b. that they must build a large hollow wooden horse to invade Persia
    c. that they must gather their warships to attack the Persian armada (*)
    d. that a defense of Greece was hopeless

23. Which inscription was *not* on the facade of the temple at Delphi?
    a. "Love Your Neighbor" (*)
    b. "Know Yourself"
    c. "Nothing in Excess"
    d. "Govern Your Spirit"

24. How did Apollo acquire priests for his temple at Delphi, according to the *Hymn to Pythian Apollo*?
    a. He created them out of laurel trees.
    b. He hijacked a ship full of sailors from Crete. (*)
    c. He cut up the dead Python and created priests from its parts.
    d. There is no account of such an event in the hymn.

25. In what shape did Apollo approach the Cretan ship?
    a. as Poseidon
    b. as a dolphin (*)
    c. as himself
    d. as a tuna

26. What happened to Daphne?
    a. She was transformed into a laurel tree as punishment for rejecting Apollo's advances.
    b. She was transformed into a cyprus because she was grieving over her pet stag.
    c. She had a child fathered by Apollo, the first physician Asclepius.
    d. She was transformed into a laurel tree to escape Apollo's advances. (*)

27. What happened to Asclepius?
    a. He became so great a physician that he learned to revive the dead, so Zeus killed him. (*)
    b. He became so great a physician that he learned to make men give birth, so Hera killed him.
    c. He rejected the love of Athene and was killed by her sword.
    d. He became so great a blacksmith that he forged an unbreakable sword for Athene, so she awarded him by making him immortal.

28. What is sympathetic magic? Choose the most precise definition.
    a. magic performed by someone who does not want to harm you
    b. a ritual acting out what one wants to take place (*)
    c. a ritual transfer of the powers of a part onto the whole
    d. magic involving feelings, not reason

ESSAY QUESTIONS

29. Explain the following sentence: "Setting the example of a god who performs slave labor to purge himself of guilt, Apollo creates a paradigm of expiation for mortals who later seek to cleanse themselves of error."

30. Give an etiological explanation of the myth of Daphne, linking it to the rituals at Delphi.

31. Discuss why myth presents Apollo as almost always suffering erotic rejection and loss.

CHAPTER 8
DIONYSUS: ROOTED IN EARTH AND ECSTASY

TRUE/FALSE QUESTIONS

1. Each summer Dionysus resided in Delphi for three months while Apollo was up North to escape the heat. (F)

2. There is a theory that Apollo and Dionysus are actually two aspects of the same divinity. (T)

3. Dionysus is commonly identified with other male fertility gods of the ancient Near East: Tammutz (Dumuzi), Adonis, and Osiris. (T)

4. Dionysus is generally identified in myths as a true "native son": his origin is exclusively Greek. (F)

5. Dionysus's mother is persuaded by Hera that her lover, whom she has never seen, is really Zeus, so she demands to know the truth. When she learns that Hera was right, she dies from the shock. (F)

6. Dionysus is born from his father's castrated genitals, which had been thrown into the sea. (F)

7. Dionysus is a fertility god representing the growth, death, and rebirth of vegetation. (T)

8. Semele's sister Ino tries to protect Dionysus by disguising him as a goat. (F)

9. Icarius is murdered while he is wearing the skin of a goat. (T)

10. Satyrs are famous for their physical strength and are often depicted with exaggeratedly large muscles. (F)

11. Orpheus renounces women after having failed to bring his wife Eurydice back from the land of the dead. (T)

12. Orpheus was the victim of sparagmos. (T)

13. Orphism includes the idea of reincarnation. (T)

14. Orphism promotes an alternative version of the Dionysian myth in which humans are created from the ashes of the Titans who killed and ate Dionysus. (T)

15. Orphism promotes an alternative version of the Dionysian myth which humans are born from the dolphins who abducted and ate Dionysus. (F)

16. The Dionysian Mysteries were very popular in Greece and Italy and persisted well into the Christian era. (T)

17. Orphism created a balance between Dionysian excess and Apollonian moderation. (T)

18. Early Christians used the figure of Orpheus or Dionysus to depict Jesus. (T)

19. In the *Hymn to Dionysus,* pirates try to capture Dionysus, who has taken on the disguise of a dolphin. (F)

20. In the *Hymn to Dionysus,* Dionysus utilizes the shapes of a lion and a bear. (T)

MULTIPLE-CHOICE QUESTIONS

21. Apollo and Dionysus have several qualities in common except which one of the following?
    a. Both were born under difficult circumstances, persecuted by Hera.
    b. Both are associated with ecstasy.
    c. Both share their father Zeus's will to power.
    d. Both have female as well as male elements in their nature. (*)

22. Dionysus shares certain characteristics with other male fertility gods of the ancient Near East except which one of the following?
    a. They all undergo a violent death.
    b. They all undergo dismemberment and are ritually eaten. (*)
    c. They all descend into the Underworld.
    d. They all are reborn as immortal beings.

23. What causes the death of Semele?
    a. She is persuaded by Hera that her lover, whom she has never seen, is really Zeus, so she demands to know the truth. When she learns that Hera was right, she dies of shock.
    b. Hera convinces Semele that her lover who visits her in the dark is an ogre. Semele persuades her lover to show himself as he really is, and when Zeus appears in a blaze of light, she is incinerated. (*)
    c. She has spurned the advances of Zeus and is struck down with his thunderbolt.
    d. Being a mortal woman, she grows old and dies, and nothing her lover Zeus can do will make her young again.

24. How did Ampelus die?
    a. He was transformed into a grapevine.
    b. He was gored by a raging bull. (*)
    c. He was transformed into a dolphin.
    d. He was murdered by shepherds who thought he was a goat.

25. Who was Icarius?
    a. Dionysus's first lover
    b. Dionysus's last lover
    c. the man Dionysus taught to manufacture wine (*)
    d. the leader of the pirates who tried to abduct Dionysus

26. What trait does Orpheus *not* share with Dionysus?
    a. bisexuality
    b. a descent into Hades
    c. a violent death
    d. being the son of Zeus (*)

27. What does *soma sema* mean? Pick the most likely translation.
    a. "The body is a prison." (*)
    b. "The soul resides in man's seed."
    c. "Ashes to ashes, dust to dust."
    d. "From cradle to grave."

28. What happens when pirates attempt to kidnap Dionysus?
    a. He changes them into dolphins. (*)
    b. He becomes a dolphin and escapes them.
    c. He attacks the ship with the help of dolphins.
    d. Trick question: Dolphins try to kidnap him and are, as punishment, changed into pirates.

29. What is a thyrsus?
    a. an older Greek word for the ritual of sparagmos
    b. a ritual of sacred intercourse to promote fertility
    c. a long staff topped with a pinecone and entwined with ivy (*)
    d. a staff topped with wings and entwined by two snakes

30. Who is Dionysus Zagreus?
    a. another name for Orpheus
    b. a name for the Orphic variation of the Dionysus myth (*)
    c. a name for the Apollonian aspect of Dionysus
    d. a Slavic version of the Dionysus myth, first encountered in the region of Zagreb

ESSAY QUESTIONS

31. Give an explanation of the goat theme in the Dionysus cult in terms of (1) an etiological theory and (2) a psychological theory.

32. Specify the Orphic variations in Dionysus's myth, and explain how his cult is linked to Orphism.

33. Explain the similarities and differences between Orpheus, Dionysus, and Apollo.

CHAPTER 9

LAND OF NO RETURN:
THE GLOOMY KINGDOM OF HADES

TRUE/FALSE QUESTIONS

1. When Odysseus learns that he must descend into Hades's realm, he feels intense curiosity and excitement. (F)

2. In the Underworld, Achilles tells Odysseus that he would rather be king of the dead than a poor man's living slave. (F)

3. The souls in Hades have lost memory, reason, and willpower. (T)

4. Odysseus performs a ritual to summon the dead and communicate with them by preparing for them a sacrificial meal consisting of animal skins and bones. (F)

5. The ancient Hebrew netherworld resembles the Homeric Hades: the dead inhabit an underground region of inactivity, regardless of whether they have been good or evil in life. (T)

6. In Homeric tradition, drinking from the river Lethe made you forget your previous life. (F)

7. The Homeric Elysium is a form of paradise awaiting all good Greeks when they die. (F)

8. Hades is also a place for monsters like Pluto, the hound from hell. (F)

9. It was a Greek custom to bury people with coins in their hands or mouth to pay the ferryman Cerberus to ferry them across to Hades. (F)

10. Morpheus (the god of sleep) and his son Hypnos (the god of dreams) also live in Hades. (F)

11. Hypnos (sleep) is the brother of Thanatos (death). (T)

12. Tityus's punishment is to suffer thirst and hunger but never to be able to reach water or food. (F)

13. Sisyphus must roll a boulder uphill, watch it roll down, and roll it back up again in eternity because he smart-talked his way out of Hades once before. (T)

14. A heroic journey to the Underworld and back is known as a katabasis. (T)

15. Heracles traveled to the Underworld to steal a dog. (T)

16. Orpheus didn't succeed in bringing Eurydice back to life because he was tricked by Hermes. (F)

17. According to early Christian writers, Jesus entered the netherworld on Good Friday to retrieve righteous souls who died before he had opened the way to heaven. (T)

18. The Homeric view of Hades can be compared to a Freudian or Jungian dreamlike state of paralysis. (T)

19. Greek philosophers came to believe that souls were dealt with after death according to whether they were good or evil in life. (T)

20. Virgil portrays Odysseus's descent into the land of the dead as an exploration of the human subconscious. (F)

MULTIPLE-CHOICE QUESTIONS

21. Who is the brother of Thanatos?
    a. Hades
    b. Minos
    c. Morpheus
    d. Hypnos (*)

22. What is the name of the hound from hell?
    a. Plato
    b. Pluto
    c. Charon
    d. Cerberus (*)

23. There are three explanations why Tantalus received his punishment. Which is not one of those explanations?
    a. He stole ambrosia from the gods and gave it to humans.
    b. He stole fire from the gods and gave it to humans. (*)
    c. He divulged secret divine tabletalk.
    d. He served up his son as food for the gods.

24. Why did Hades and Persephone agree to let Orpheus try to bring his wife back from the dead?
    a. They were moved by his music. (*)
    b. They were moved by his tears.
    c. It was an evil scheme: They had no intentions of letting him get away with it.
    d. They were moved by his beautiful smile.

25. Why did Heracles descend into the Underworld?
    a. to rescue his mother Semele and make her immortal
    b. to kidnap the hound from hell (*)
    c. to speak to the wisest of the dead, Tiresias
    d. to rescue his beloved wife, dead from a snake-bite

26. What is the term for a heroic descent into the Underworld?
   a. calabasas
   b. sparagmos
   c. katabasis (*)
   d. hieros gamos

27. What is meant by "the harrowing of hell"?
   a. Jesus descending to the land of the dead on Good Friday to collect the good souls (*)
   b. the rape and abduction of Persephone by Hades
   c. Orpheus playing his music in Hades and moving everyone to tears
   d. Demeter descending into Hades to fetch Persephone back

ESSAY QUESTIONS

28. Why does the fact of death cast a shadow over the efforts of Greek heroes to be immortalized through great acts of cunning and bravery?

29. Explain the differences and similarities between the Homeric Hades and Tartarus of the later Greek tradition.

30. Explain the descent of a Greek or Roman hero into the Underworld in terms of a Freudian or Jungian theory of myth.

CHAPTER 10

THE HERO: MAN DIVIDED AGAINST HIMSELF

TRUE/FALSE QUESTIONS

1. Perseus is the quintessential Greek hero, performing heroic tasks and having severe problems relating to women. (F)

2. Perseus's mother was imprisoned by her husband in his jealousy over her relationship with Zeus. (F)

3. When Perseus offers to bring King Polydectes any gift of his choice as a substitute for his mother, Polydectes demands the head of Medusa. (T)

4. Medusa is one of the three Graeae. (F)

5. In Freudian theory, decapitation is an unconscious image of castration. (T)

6. Through the magic eye of the Graeae, Perseus sees that Andromeda is in trouble and rushes to save her. (F)

7. Following his return, Perseus accidentally kills his grandfather with a discus throw. (T)

8. Abandoned by Perseus, Andromeda kills their two children and herself. (F)

9. Heracles is the parthenogenic son of Hera. (F)

10. One of Heracles's Twelve Labors is bringing back the girdle of the Amazon Queen Hippolyte. (T)

11. The Twelve Labors are Heracles's punishment for killing his wife Medea, after she killed their two children. (F)

12. Even if Heracles is several generations older than Jason, he still joins Jason and the Argonauts on their voyage. (T)

13. Theseus's father kills himself because he erroneously assumes that his son is dead. (T)

14. Like Perseus and his Andromeda, Theseus settles down to a happy marriage with the woman he loves, Ariadne. (F)

15. Jason is raised by the same centaur who taught Asclepius the art of medicine. (T)

16. As a condition for giving Jason the fleece, the king of Colchis demands that he sow a field with dragon's teeth and fight the dragons that germinate from the teeth. (F)

17. Medea kills and dismembers her younger brother, tossing the pieces into the sea so that her father will be delayed by funeral rituals. (T)

18. Icarus, son of Daedalus, is given a pair of wax wings by his father so that they can escape the wrath of King Minos after Daedalus helped Theseus. (T)

19. The moral of the story of Phaethon: being half-divine does not grant you divine powers. (T)

20. When invited to the wedding of a Sabine princess, the centaurs drink too much and try to rape and carry off the Sabine women. (F)

MULTIPLE-CHOICE QUESTIONS

21. Perseus receives three magical weapons to slay Medusa. Which one does he not receive?
    a. a pair of winged sandals
    b. a sword that cuts through stone (*)
    c. a cape of invisibility
    d. a pouch

22. How does Perseus avoid being turned into stone by Medusa?
    a. He closes his eyes when she turns around and then cuts off her head.
    b. He looks at her reflection in his shield and then cuts off her head. (*)
    c. He throws the magic pouch over her head and then cuts it off.
    d. He approaches her flying backward on his winged sandals, closes his eyes as he turns, and cuts off her head.

23. The most characteristic traits of Heracles are listed here. Which of the following is not one of them?
    a. He is capable of animal-like behavior.
    b. He is unnaturally brave and strong.
    c. He is extremely cunning and wise. (*)
    d. He is protective of society.

24. How did Heracles die?
    a. A ship's beam fell on his head and killed him.
    b. He was pushed or fell down a cliff to his death, mimicking the death of his own father.
    c. His wife made an ointment that was supposed to ensure his commitment to her, but the ointment ate through his skin and killed him. (*)
    d. Trick question: he is a god and cannot die.

25. Why did Theseus go to Crete?
    a. He was captured and sent to Crete as a sacrifice to the Minotaur, and nobody believed he was the son of the king.
    b. He volunteered as a sacrifice in order to stop the killing of young Athenian men and women. (*)
    c. He had been told by the Oracle at Delphi that a great love waited for him on Crete.
    d. He went in order to rescue Ariadne, who was to be sacrificed.

26. General characteristics shared by Greek heroes do not include which one of the following?
    a. having an animallike nature (*)
    b. having divine ancestors
    c. having problems with women
    d. dying a nonheroic death

27. Who was Pelias?
    a. Jason's father
    b. the half-divine son of Helios
    c. Jason's uncle (*)
    d. Theseus's father

28. How does Medea try to delay her father's pursuit of the *Argos*?
    a. She kills and dismembers her younger brother, and serves him up for her father with a powerful poison.
    b. She kills and dismembers her younger brother, tossing the pieces into the sea so that her father will be delayed by funeral rituals. (*)
    c. She kills her two children and sends their bodies by messenger to her father, blaming Jason.
    d. She kills and dismembers Jason's uncle as a warning to her father.

29. Why do the wax wings of Icarus fail him?
    a. because his father suffered from *hubris*, overconfidence at his own invention
    b. because he didn't listen to his father's advice of moderation in flight (*)
    c. because Hera had put a spell on him, being angry that Theseus had escaped the Minotaur
    d. trick question: it wasn't Icarus whose wings melted—it was his father, Daedalus.

30. What lesson are we supposed to learn from the story of Phaethon?
    a. Being half-divine does not grant you divine powers. (*)
    b. Being strong does not guarantee that you are also wise.
    c. A job worth doing is worth doing well.
    d. Moderation is a virtue.

ESSAY QUESTIONS

31. In what ways is Perseus similar to Heracles and Theseus, and how does he differ from them?

32. What is the psychological interpretation of Heracles's death caused by his wife's attempt to make him commit to her?

33. Does Jason also undergo a rite of passage? Explain Jason's journey in terms of the archetypal pattern of separation and initiation.

CHAPTER 11
HEROES AT WAR: THE TROY SAGA

TRUE/FALSE QUESTIONS

1. Zeus has arranged a wedding between Thetis, a minor sea goddess, and a mortal man, Peleus; at this wedding, problems arise that will result in the Trojan War. (T)

2. Zeus invites to the wedding all the gods and goddesses except Aphrodite, the goddess of love. (F)

3. Paris gives the apple to Aphrodite in exchange for her love. (F)

4. Helen was exceedingly beautiful because she was the daughter of Zeus. (T)

5. Greek myths are essentially closed-ended, having a beginning, a middle, and an ending. (F)

6. Thetis tries to immortalize her son Achilles by dipping him in the waters of the Nile, holding him by his heel. (F)

7. The Homeric gods have complete power over human destinies. (F)

8. According to Homer, humans have, in a limited sense, freedom to act but must bear the responsibility of their actions. (T)

9. Homer may have lived on an island off the coast of Sicily between 1100 and 1000 B.C. (F)

10. The *Iliad* and the *Odyssey* may have been written or edited by different poets. (T)

11. Both the *Iliad* and the *Odyssey* are composed with dialogue and an omniscient narrator. (T)

12. Contrary to the myth, the epic is rooted in human time. (T)

13. The heroes of the *Iliad* are divided beings: they must be social beings, because it is their nature, but this means that they must violate their needs as warriors. (F)

14. Achilles has two possible fates: a long life in obscurity or a short, brilliant one in battle. (T)

15. Diomedes is the image of a moderate hero. (T)

16. The gods take sides: Apollo, Artemis, and Aphrodite side with the Greeks, and Hera, Poseidon, and Athene favor the Trojans. (F)

17. Achilles's dual destinies show that fate is not predetermined but conditional. (T)

18. The two urns from which Zeus doles out gifts are the image of the human condition: Some receive exclusively from the urn of happiness, and some only from the urn of unhappiness; most receive half from each. (F)

19. The Greeks who represent family values have abandoned their own families to go to war, while the transgressors of family values, the Trojans, are depicted as ideal models of family love. (T)

20. Achilles undergoes a rite of passage just like other heroes, but for him it is an internal journey. (T)

MULTIPLE-CHOICE QUESTIONS

21. Which of these goddesses did not take part in the quarrel over the golden apple?
     a. Athene
     b. Artemis (*)
     c. Aphrodite
     d. Hera

22. There is a chronological problem in the *Iliad*; what is it?
     a. Since Paris is the son of Peleus and Hecuba, he is too young to have been present at the Trojan War.
     b. Since Achilles is the son of Peleus and Thetis, he is too young to have been present at the Trojan War. (*)
     c. Since Paris has killed Achilles's son in battle, Achilles is too old to have been a young hero at Troy.
     d. Since Andromache's father was killed by Achilles, he is too old to have been present at Troy.

23. What is an "Achilles's heel"?
     a. a point of vulnerability (*)
     b. a hero gone bad, like Achilles
     c. a secret weapon: the Greek athlete's kick
     d. another word for winged sandals

24. What is the speculation as to where and when Homer lived?
     a. in Athens, fifth century B.C.
     b. on an island off the coast of Sicily between 1100 and 1000 B.C.
     c. on an island off the coast of Asia Minor, between 800 and 700 B.C. (*)
     d. in Macedonia during the ninth century B.C.

25. Both the *Iliad* and the *Odyssey* contain formal literary conventions. Which one is not such a convention?
     a. the proem
     b. the katabasis of the hero
     c. the semidivinity of the hero
     d. the sparagmos of the hero (*)

26. Why must the Trojans lose the war?
    a. because Zeus has sided with the Greeks from the beginning
    b. because the Trojans have broken the rules of courtesy, the sanctity of the family, and the guest-host relationship (*)
    c. because the Trojans, having loving family relationships, are essentially effeminate compared to the extreme masculinity of the Greeks
    d. because humans have no free will; everything has been predetermined since the dawn of time

27. Who, according to the textbook, are the real victims of the Trojan War?
    a. the Trojans
    b. the slaves
    c. the children
    d. the women (*)

28. What does it mean that Hector and Achilles can't acknowledge their anima?
    a. They can't come to terms with the feminine side of themselves. (*)
    b. They can't come to terms with the masculine side of themselves.
    c. They can't come to terms with the idea of imminent death.
    d. They can't come to terms with the concept of an immortal soul.

29. What is the final scene in the *Iliad*?
    a. the Trojan Horse being dragged inside the city of Troy
    b. the battle for the city ensuing after the deception of the Trojan Horse
    c. Hector's funeral (*)
    d. Hector's death

30. Who is Patroclus?
    a. the brother of Hector
    b. the close friend of Achilles (*)
    c. the son of Peleus and Thetis
    d. the husband of Andromache

ESSAY QUESTIONS

31. Give an explanation according to a Freudian or Jungian theory of Eris's appearance at the wedding of Thetis and Peleus.

32. Compare the Greeks' and Trojans' attitudes toward the family, using specific examples from the *Iliad*.

33. Compare Achilles and Hector: How are they alike? In what ways do they differ?

34.   Comment on the following passage: What is happening, and who are involved?

> They passed the lookout point, the wild figtree
> with wind in all its leaves, then veered away
> along the curving wagon road, and came
> to where the double fountains well, the source
> of eddying Skamander. One hot spring
> flows out, and from the water fumes arise
> as though from fire burning: but the other even in summer gushes chill
>   as hail
> or snow or crystal ice frozen on water.
> Near these fountains are wide washing pools
> of smooth-laid stone, where Trojan wives and daughters
> laundered their smooth linen in the days
> of peace before the Akhaians came. Past these
> the two men ran, pursuer and pursued,
> and he who fled was noble, he behind
> a greater man by far

35.   Explain the following passage and comment about (1) its connection with the previous passage and (2) how it illustrates the Homeric outlook on life and the personal character of the men involved.

> "I beg you by your soul and by your parents,
> do not let the dogs feed on me
> in your encampment by the ships. Accept
> the bronze and gold my father will provide
> as gifts, my father and her ladyship
> my mother. Let them have my body back,
> so that our men and women may accord me
> decency of fire when I am dead."
> Akhilleus the great runner scowled and said:
> "Beg me no beggary by soul or parents,
> whining dog! Would god my passion drove me
> to slaughter you and eat you raw, you've caused
> such agony to me! No man exists
> who could defend you from the carrion pack—
> not if they spread for me ten times your ransom,
> twenty times, and promise more as well;
> aye, not if Priam, son of Dardanos,
> tells them to buy you for your weight in gold!
> You'll have no bed of death, nor will you be
> laid out and mourned by her who gave you birth.
> Dogs and birds will have you, every scrap."

CHAPTER 12

A DIFFERENT KIND OF HERO:
THE QUEST OF ODYSSEUS

TRUE/FALSE QUESTIONS

1. Some modern critics assume that the *Odyssey*'s author is a woman. (T)

2. Odysseus does not appear until book 5 of the *Odyssey*. (T)

3. The *Odyssey* begins with the confrontation between Odysseus and his father Laertes, which causes Odysseus to go off to war to seek honor for himself. (F)

4. The first event of Odysseus's journey home is his raid on Ismarus. (T)

5. The moral universe of the *Odyssey* is typically Greek: humans have no control over their destinies; everyone is the victim of the whims of the gods. (F)

6. Agamemnon was slain by his wife's lover Orestes and avenged by his son Aegistus. (F)

7. Odysseus blinded Polyphemus, because he had said lewd things about Odysseus's wife. (F)

8. Odysseus told Polyphemus that his name was No-one. (T)

9. Calypso offers immortality to Odysseus, but Odysseus would rather go home to his wife. (T)

10. Polyphemus is the son of Helios, the sun god, who avenges him by not allowing Odysseus to travel by day. (F)

11. Odysseus built his and Penelope's marriage bed so that it could not be moved. (T)

12. Scylla was a maelstrom, while Carybdis was a monster with six heads. (F)

13. Circe made Odysseus's men drink a potion which turned them into dogs. (F)

14. Circe became Odysseus's lover for one year. (T)

15. Odysseus arrived home with only three men from his original crew. (F)

16. Lord Tennyson interprets Odysseus as embodying a modern spirit of scientific heroism. (T)

17. Calypso is the Muse who inspires composers of rhythmic music. (F)

18. Penelope delayed her suitors by weaving a piece of cloth by day and unraveling it by night. (T)

19. Odysseus loses his men because they killed and ate the sacred cattle of Poseidon. (F)

20. In order for the dead in Hades to speak, Odysseus must feed them blood. (T)

MULTIPLE-CHOICE QUESTIONS

21. Several traits distinguish Odysseus from other Greek heroes. Which one is not one of them?
    a. He has fully human parents.
    b. He uses cunning rather than brute force.
    c. He descends into the Underworld. (*)
    d. He does not die young, but lives a long life.

22. Why does Odysseus descend into the Underworld?
    a. to speak to his mother one more time
    b. to seek advice from the blind seer Tiresias (*)
    c. to seek advice from Achilles
    d. to ask his young friend Elpenor how he wants to be buried

23. Why does Agamemnon tell Odysseus in the Underworld not to trust his wife?
    a. because Agamemnon was killed by his wife and her lover (*)
    b. because Agamemnon's mother killed his father
    c. because he knows Penelope has been unfaithful to Odysseus
    d. because he hates all women

24. How does Hermes help Odysseus against Circe?
    a. He gives him a cape of invisibility.
    b. He changes his appearance to that of a woman.
    c. He gives him a sword that will kill a god.
    d. He gives him an herb to mix with her potion. (*)

25. Why was Odysseus so moved to see his mother in Hades?
    a. because he did not know that she was dead (*)
    b. because he had parted with her in anger without saying goodbye
    c. because he wanted to bring her back in order to make her immortal
    d. because he had never known his mother while she was alive

ESSAY QUESTIONS

26. What is meant by Penelope embodying Odysseus's anima?

27. What is meant by Odysseus choosing his home and his wife rather than immortality with Calypso? Be specific.

28. Explain the following passage in terms of its context within the *Odyssey* and its outlook on the human condition.

> " 'Achilles, neither past nor future holds
> a man more blessed than you. In life indeed
> we Argives honored you as deity;
> and now, among the dead, you are supreme.
> In death you have no need to grieve, Achilles.'
>
> "These were my words. He did not wait to answer:
> 'Odysseus, don't embellish death for me.
> I'd rather be another's hired hand,
> working for some poor man who owns no land
> but pays his rent from what scant gains he gets,
> than to rule over all whom death has crushed.' "

29. Explain the point of this line by Penelope:

> "Prepare the sturdy bedstead for him now
> outside the solid bridal room that he
> himself constructed; carry out the bed,
> and over it throw cloaks, bright blankets, fleece."

CHAPTER 13

THE THEATER OF DIONYSUS
AND THE TRAGIC VISION

TRUE/FALSE QUESTIONS

1. The German philosopher Friedrich Nietzsche argued that Greek art reached its perfection with the realization that Apollonian and Dionysian forces could not be reconciled, thus giving birth to the genre of Apollonian tragedy and Dionysian comedy. (F)

2. The philosopher Friedrich Nietzsche argued that Greek art reached its creative peak in the Greek tragedy where the Apollonian sense of distinct identity and the Dionysian passion form a synthesis. (T)

3. The Great Dionysia were held for five days in October, celebrating the making of new wine. (F)

4. The Dionysia staged three different kinds of plays— tragedy, comedy, and satyr plays. (T)

5. The first winner of the tragic competition was Thespis. (T)

6. The first rule of the tragedy was that the protagonist had to be Dionysus himself. (F)

7. Aristotle viewed the tragedy as a cleansing emotional experience for the audience. (T)

8. The main content of the satyr plays was humorous antics and obscene jokes. (T)

9. Comedies had their own festival. (T)

10. The tragic hero has a capacity for extremes of feeling and behavior, which contradicts the Apollonian awareness of one's human limitations. (T)

11. In drama as well as in the epic, a narrative voice guides the perception of the audience. (F)

12. In the tragic drama, the protagonists are more realistic than in the myths. (T)

13. The tragic hero is doomed to suffer, because he or she is trapped between conflicting demands. (T)

14. The tragic quest is typically an external journey of suffering, contrary to the quest of the myth, which is usually internal. (F)

15. Even though the tragic universe is ruled by divine beings, the universe is anthropocentric. (T)

16. In the tragic universe, there is still divine justice waiting at the conclusion of the story. (F)

17. Aristotle says that *peripeteia* defines the tragic experience. (T)

MULTIPLE-CHOICE QUESTIONS

18. What is the origin of the word *tragedy*?
    a. a goat play
    b. a parade of revelers
    c. a goat song (*)
    d. a sad song

19. Most satyr plays have been lost. Why?
    a. They were met with Christian disapproval. (*)
    b. They were never written down, but survived for centuries as part of an oral ritual.
    c. They were met with public disapproval almost from the beginning.
    d. They were stored in the Dionysus temple, which burned down.

20. What is the origin of the word comedy?
    a. a parade of satyrs
    b. a parade of revelers (*)
    c. a goat-song
    d. a parade of goats

21. What is *peripeteia*?
    a. reversal (*)
    b. Wanderlust (the urge to travel)
    c. unimportant things
    d. rehearsal

22. What does the word *catharsis* mean?
    a. the hero's descent into the Underworld
    b. a cleansing (*)
    c. a hound from hell
    d. a reconciliation of opposites

23. What is meant by the phrase "the tragic universe is not morally neat"?
    a. There is no Christian value system.
    b. There is no assured divine justice. (*)
    c. There are no gods.
    d. Humans are considered evil by nature.

24. Who wrote the tragedy the *Bacchants*?
    a. Sophocles
    b. Aristophanes
    c. Euripides (*)
    d. Aeschylus

Chapter 13   The Theater of Dionysus and the Tragic Vision   137

ESSAY QUESTIONS

25. What did Aristotle mean by calling the experience of a tragedy *cathartic*? Define the term, discuss Aristotle's idea, and relate it to current debates about the values and dangers of entertainment.

26. Explain and comment on the following sentence: "Often culminating in a sudden access of insight beyond the limits of ordinary sense experience, the tragic hero's experience corresponds loosely with the epiphany and consequent communion of the Dionysian ritual."

27. Discuss the similarities and differences between tragic and epic heroes.

CHAPTER 14

COSMIC CONFLICT AND EVOLUTION: AESCHYLUS'S TRANSFORMATION OF THE PROMETHEUS MYTH

TRUE/FALSE QUESTIONS

1. In spite of their audiences being largely similar, Hesiod and Aeschylus wrote remarkably different plays about Prometheus. (F)

2. Aeschylus was a veteran of several battles against the Persians. (T)

3. Aeschylus had been the Greek leader at the Battle of Salamis. (F)

4. The democracy of Athens had been established some twenty years before the Persian invasion began. (T)

5. Except for the comedies of Aristophanes, all Greek plays were written between the end of the Persian Wars and the deaths of Sophocles and Euripides. (T)

6. Most of Aeschylus's plays dealt with contemporary history. (F)

7. Aeschylus interprets Prometheus as a tyrant, whereas Hesiod sees him as a heroic rebel. (F)

8. Zeus, in Aeschylus's interpretation, is omnipotent as well as omniscient. (F)

9. *Prometheus Bound* is the first part of a trilogy; the other two parts remain only in fragments: *Prometheus Unbound* and *Prometheus the Fire-Eater*. (F)

10. Zeus allows Heracles to kill the eagle that is feasting on Prometheus's liver. (T)

11. The poet Shelley interpreted Prometheus as an image of the human mind, remaining free despite its physical bondage. (T)

12. Aeschylus's interpretation of Prometheus reflects the Greek ambivalence toward an individualism that may disrupt social order. (T)

13. Hesiod claims that Prometheus is a second-generation Titan; Aeschylus identifies him as a son of Gaea. (T)

14. *Hubris* means to "miss the mark" when target shooting. (F)

15. Prometheus's virtue of intellectual honesty brings about his suffering. (T)

16. The young woman Io was being stung by a gadfly sent by Hermes. (F)

17. The chorus sides with Prometheus against Hermes and Zeus, although the Greek chorus usually takes a mediating position. (T)

18. Prometheus's defiance gives Zeus an opportunity to save himself from a future downfall at the hands of Prometheus's son. (F)

19. Because of an oath sworn by Zeus that he wouldn't release Prometheus, the Titan must wear a fragment of the rock attached to a steel ring. (T)

MULTIPLE-CHOICE QUESTIONS

20. How long before the Persian invasion of Greece was the Athenian democracy established?
     a. twenty years (*)
     b. five years
     c. fifty years
     d. seventy-five years

21. Why might Zeus's reconciliation with Prometheus be compared to his swallowing of Metis?
     a. Both are false reconciliations: Zeus does not allow for anyone to best him; he would rather swallow them up.
     b. Both are examples of true, bonding love: you absorb the one you love.
     c. Both are examples of Zeus assimilating the qualities of the other. (*)
     d. The comparison is mistaken; there is no common ground.

22. Why did Prometheus give the fire to humans, according to Aeschylus?
     a. to spite the gods
     b. to alleviate human suffering (*)
     c. in response to a wager with Hermes
     d. by accident, accentuating Zeus's lack of a sense of justice

23. What quality brings about the suffering of Prometheus?
     a. his virtue of intellectual honesty (*)
     b. his virtue of divine courage
     c. his virtue of modesty
     d. his virtue of divine curiosity

24. Aeschylus wrote a trilogy about Prometheus. What was the title of the third play?
     a. *Prometheus the Fire-Eater*
     b. *Prometheus the Fire-Bearer* (*)
     c. *Prometheus the Fire-Man*
     d. *Prometheus the Fire-Stealer*

25. What does *hamartia* mean?
     a. "overconfidence"
     b. "missing the mark" (*)
     c. "I have found it!"
     d. "All artists are hams"

26. In his conversation with Hermes, Prometheus utters the following remark: "Two dynasties I have seen fall from heaven, and I shall see the third fall faster, most shamefully of all." What is he referring to?
   a. a prophecy of the fall of Athens to Sparta in 404 B.C.
   b. a prophecy of the fall of Cronus at the hands of Zeus
   c. a prophecy of the fall of Greece to Persia, a prophecy that never came true
   d. a prophecy of the fall of Zeus to a stronger son, a prophecy that never came true (*)

ESSAY QUESTIONS

27. Explain Ocean's function in *Prometheus Bound*: What is his viewpoint, and how does Prometheus react to his advice?

28. Explain the following passage from *Prometheus Bound*:

> Hear rather all that mortals suffered.
> Once they were fools. I gave them power to think.
> Through me they won their minds.
> I have no blame for them. All I would tell you
> is my good will and my good gifts to them.
> Seeing they did not see, nor hearing hear.
> Like dreams they led a random life.
> They had no houses built to face the sun,
> of bricks or well-wrought wood,
> but like the tiny ant who has her home
> in sunless crannies deep down in the earth,
> they lived in caverns . . .
> . . . From me they learned the stars that tell the seasons,
> their risings and their settings hard to mark.
> And number, that most excellent device,
> I taught to them, and letters joined in words.
> I gave to them the mother of all arts,
> hard-working memory.

29. Discuss the specific ways in which Aeschylus's depiction of Prometheus differs from Hesiod's.

30. Describe Io's function in the play.

CHAPTER 15

THE HOUSE OF ATREUS: AESCHYLUS'S *ORESTEIA*

TRUE/FALSE QUESTIONS

1. Aeschylus's *Oresteia* is one of only three surviving complete trilogies of Greek tragedy. (F)

2. As in the *Prometheus* trilogy, Aeschylus explores the Greek belief that the gods are not unchangeable. (T)

3. The first play, the *Agamemnon*, opens in Argos shortly before Agamemnon's departure for Troy. (F)

4. The third part of the trilogy, the *Eumenides*, features Orestes seeking purification at Delphi. (T)

5. Aeschylus did not write only tragedies; he also wrote a satyr play about Menelaus. (T)

6. The main point in the *Eumenides* is the transformation of the Gorgons into priestesses of Apollo at Delphi. (F)

7. Agamemnon is related to Tantalus, who is condemned to roll a rock uphill in Hades only to watch it roll down again and again. (F)

8. Agamemnon's father, Atreus, repeats his ancestor Tantalus's crime of serving a dismembered human being as food. (T)

9. Before leaving Argos for Troy, Agamemnon sacrifices his daughter Iphigenia to the gods. (T)

10. Cassandra, a Trojan priestess of Apollo, is cursed with a clairvoyance that nobody believes. (T)

11. Clytemnestra kills Cassandra because she has foretold that Clytemnestra is going to kill Agamemnon. (F)

12. In Aeschylus's version, Agamemnon is killed by Clytemnestra and her lover working together as a team. (F)

13. Clytemnestra is a representative of the Great Goddess, showing solidarity with other women in the face of patriarchal pressure. (F)

14. In the *Libation-Bearers,* Orestes has to decide whether to obey Apollo's order to avenge his father by slaying his mother, and incur the wrath of the Furies. (T)

15. The *Oresteia* identifies the feminine principle with the powers of darkness. (T)

16. Apollo declares that a mother is merely an incubator for the seed that the father deposits in her. (T)

17. In the Homeric version of the story of Agamemnon, the king is killed by his wife's lover, Aegisthus. (T)

18. Prior to Aeschylus, the story of Agamemnon and Orestes usually illustrated a competition for power between gods and humans. (F)

19. Because Cassandra refused to follow Apollo's command of becoming the lover of Agamemnon, he cursed her with clairvoyance. (F)

20. The Furies are the same as the Gorgons. (F)

MULTIPLE-CHOICE QUESTIONS

21. Choose another word for the Furies:
    a. the Gorgons
    b. the Erinyes (*)
    c. the Fates
    d. the Moiras

22. Which title does not belong to the trilogy of the *Oresteia*?
    a. the *Pylades* (*)
    b. the *Eumenides*
    c. the *Libation-Bearers*
    d. the *Agamemnon*

23. Why is Cassandra not a successful clairvoyant?
    a. because her prophecies do not come true
    b. because she is unable to voice her prophecies, due to Apollo's curse
    c. because nobody believes her prophecies, due to Apollo's curse (*)
    d. because she makes up the prophecies as she goes along without having visions

24. Who are the members of the chorus in the *Eumenides*?
    a. older citizens of Argos
    b. captive Trojan women
    c. the Furies (*)
    d. the Gorgons

25. Why does Orestes feel that he is facing a moral dilemma?
    a. because if he avenges his father, he has to kill the mother he loves
    b. because if he avenges his father and kills his mother, the Furies will kill him (*)
    c. because if he avenges his father and kills his mother, Apollo will kill him
    d. because if he avenges his father and kills his mother, his sister Electra will have to kill him

26. What, according to Aeschylus, is the main point of the third part of the *Oresteia*?
     a. the transformation of the Furies into a socially stabilizing power (*)
     b. the transformation of the Gorgons into a socially stabilizing power
     c. the transformation of the Gorgons into priestesses of Apollo at Delphi
     d. the transformation of the Furies from female to male spirits

27. What did King Atreus do that was reminiscent of his ancestor Tantalus?
     a. He starved to death surrounded by food and drink, which he could not digest.
     b. He killed the sons of his enemy, cooked them, and served them to his enemy without letting him know what he was eating. (*)
     c. He raped and killed a priestess of Apollo.
     d. He put his twin sons to death because of a prophecy that they would conspire to kill him.

28. In Aeschylus's version of the story, Agamemnon is murdered by
     a. Aegisthus and Clytemnestra.
     b. Aegisthus.
     c. Clytemnestra. (*)
     d. Aegisthus and Cassandra.

29. What is the factor that makes Orestes decide to kill his mother?
     a. He has a vision of the Furies.
     b. His friend Pylades reminds him of Apollo's command. (*)
     c. The ghost of his father speaks to him, revealing his mother's unfaithfulness with Orestes's uncle Aegisthus.
     d. He realizes that Clytemnestra is not his birth mother.

30. In what way might one say that Agamemnon continues the evil instigated by his ancestor, Tantalus?
     a. He sacrifices his child, Iphigenia, to the gods. (*)
     b. He sacks the city of Troy, with no concern for its holy places.
     c. He takes a woman captive and is the indirect cause of her death.
     d. He kills his brother and serves him to his father for dinner.

ESSAY QUESTIONS

31. Identify the speaker of the following passage, and evaluate his or her words: Do they make sense? Why or why not?

> But what did you do then to contravene
> *His* purpose, when, to exorcise the storms,
> As though picking a ewe-lamb from his flocks,
> Whose wealth of snowy fleeces never fails
> To increase and multiply, he killed his own
> Child, born to me in pain, my best-beloved?
> Why did you not drive *him* from hearth and home?

32. Evaluate the moral of Orestes's acquittal: How is his crime viewed by Aeschylus? Evaluate his crime from a modern, Western point of view.

33. Explain the structure of the *Eumenides,* and apply the structuralist theory of interpreting myth to the religious and social divisions embodied in the key characters.

34. Explore the similarities and differences between the *Oresteia* and Shakespeare's tragedy *Hamlet.*

CHAPTER 16

THE TRAGIC HERO: SOPHOCLES'S OEDIPUS

TRUE/FALSE QUESTIONS

1. Sophocles was a veteran of the Peloponnesian War. (F)

2. Sophocles lived through most of what is known as the classical age of Greece. (T)

3. In spite of cultural progress, the Greeks were questioning their relationship to the gods at the time of Sophocles. (T)

4. Sophocles was active in the political life of Athens. (T)

5. *Oedipus Rex* opens with a description of the plague in Athens. (F)

6. Sigmund Freud argued that every male child unconsciously desires to kill his father and marry his mother. (T)

7. Oedipus's own endeavor to find the truth can be compared with the psychoanalytic process. (T)

8. Apollo strikes Thebes with plague in order to punish Oedipus for his sins. (F)

9. Tiresias lost his sight because he had looked at the Eleusinian Mysteries without being invited. (F)

10. The sin that angers Apollo is not Oedipus's murder and incest, but the lack of civic duty displayed by the citizens of Thebes. (T)

11. The city of Thebes sided with the Persians in the Peloponnesian War. (F)

12. During his adolescence, Oedipus experienced a strong attraction toward the woman he thought of as his mother. (F)

13. Sophocles, alone of all the Greek dramatists, insisted that there is no fate; humans always have a choice. (F)

14. In *Oedipus Rex,* Oedipus thinks of himself as an innocent victim; in the later play, *Oedipus at Colonus*, Sophocles presents him as taking full responsibility for his actions, even though he acted out of ignorance. (F)

15. In *Oedipus at Colonus,* the aging Oedipus enters the cave of the Gorgons to die. (F)

16. In *Oedipus at Colonus,* Oedipus finally experiences death and transfiguration, and becomes deified in the process. (T)

17. The first play Sophocles wrote about Oedipus takes place after Oedipus's death. (T)

18. Antigone, Oedipus's daughter, is at odds with Creon, her uncle, because she insists on giving her father full funeral rites. (F)

19. For her disobedience to Creon's rule, Antigone is buried alive in a cave. (T)

20. Antigone argues that the gods are a higher authority than the state. (T)

MULTIPLE-CHOICE QUESTIONS

21. Who is saying the following, and in what context?

> If at this moment someone
> should step up to murder you.
> Would you, godly creature that you are,
> stop and say, "Excuse me, sir, are you my father?"
> Or would you deal with him then and there?

  a. Oedipus, in *Oedipus at Colonus* (*)
  b. Oedipus, in *Oedipus Rex*
  c. Theseus, in *Oedipus at Colonus*
  d. the chorus, in *Oedipus Rex*

22. Why does Apollo strike Thebes with the plague?
  a. to punish Oedipus for his sins of killing his father and marrying his mother
  b. to punish the citizens for not having caught and exiled their king's killer (*)
  c. to punish the citizens for their lack of piety in accepting the queen's son as their king.
  d. A trick question: it wasn't Thebes, but Athens.

23. Select the title of the first play written by Sophocles about Oedipus.
  a. *Oedipus at Colonus*
  b. *Oedipus Rex*
  c. *Antigone* (*)
  d. *Oedipus of Corinth*

24. The city of Thebes sided with Sparta against Athens in the following war:
  a. the Persian War
  b. the Athenian War
  c. the Trojan War
  d. the Peloponnesian War (*)

25. Why do Oedipus's sons want him to return to Thebes?
    a. The oracle says that the city that earns his goodwill will prosper after his death. (*)
    b. The oracle says that Oedipus is the only one who can solve the riddle of the Sphinx.
    c. The oracle says that only Oedipus can put an end to the plague in Thebes.
    d. They love him and miss him, even though he is their brother as well as their father.

26. In *Oedipus at Colonus*, Oedipus embraces the feminine principle by doing what?
    a. He marries a princess of Colonus.
    b. He enters the sacred cave of the Gorgons.
    c. He enters the sacred grove of the Eumenides. (*)
    d. He is reconciled with his daughters.

27. Who is Antigone trying to bury?
    a. her father, Oedipus
    b. her brother, Polynices (*)
    c. her brother, Eteocles
    d. her uncle, Creon

ESSAY QUESTIONS

28. What is the riddle of the Sphinx? What answer does Oedipus give, and how is it possible for him to give the "right" answer without fully understanding what it means?

29. Explain the significance of this passage, spoken by Jocasta in *Oedipus Rex*:

> An oracle came once to Laius. I do not say
> From Phoebus himself, but from his ministers
> That his fate would be at his son's hand to die—
> A child, who would be born from him and me.
> And yet, as the rumor says, they were strangers,
> Robbers who killed him where three highways meet.
> But three days had not passed from the child's birth
>   When Laius pierced and tied together his ankles,
> and cast him by others' hands on a pathless mountain.
> Therein Apollo did not bring to pass
> That the child murder his father, nor for Laius
> The dread he feared, to die at his son's hand.

30. Explain the following passage, identify the speaker and the context, and relate it to the Freudian theory of myth:

> What should man fear, whose life is ruled by fate,
> For whom there is clear foreknowledge of nothing?
> It is best to live by chance, however you can.
> Be not afraid of marriage with your mother;
> Already many mortals in their dreams
> Have shared their mother's bed. But he who counts
> This dream as nothing, easiest bears his life.

31. Identify the context of this passage, spoken by Oedipus: Which play does it belong to, and what is the significance of his words?

> Suppose my father by some oracle was doomed to die
> by his own son's hand,
> could you justly put the blame on me—
> a babe unborn,
> not yet begotten by a father,
> not yet engendered in a mother's womb?
> And if when born—as born I was to tragedy—
> I met my father in a fight and killed him,
> ignorant of what I did, to whom I did it,
> can you still condemn an unwilled act?

32. In what ways are the early myths about Theseus relevant to his portrayal in *Oedipus at Colonus*?

33. Does Oedipus suffer from an Oedipus complex? Explain the similarities and differences between *Oedipus Rex* and the Freudian theory.

CHAPTER 17

EURIPIDES'S *MEDEA*: A DIFFERENT PERSPECTIVE ON TRAGEDY

TRUE/FALSE QUESTIONS

1. The plays of Euripides were considered by some contemporary Athenians to be offensive. (T)

2. Medea is the daughter of Oedipus's foster parents, the king and queen of Corinth. (F)

3. Jason leaves Medea for King Creon's daughter. (T)

4. Euripides lets the chorus express the opinion that being a mother is heroic. (T)

5. Since Jason is a breaker of oaths, he is being made to suffer severely by the gods. (F)

6. In Euripides's version, Medea works through subterfuge: She lies about her evil plans, and when they are accomplished, she will not confess or take responsibility. (F)

7. Euripides uses the capacity of the drama to present multiple points of view. (T)

8. While most other female protagonists pay the price for their crimes in Greek tragedies, Medea escapes punishment. (T)

9. In Euripides's plays, the common people provide an important perspective. (T)

10. The nurse acts as Medea's accomplice in her tragic endeavor, pointing attention to the heroic qualities of the working class. (F)

11. Jason is revealed as a coward who uses women for his own gain. (T)

12. Medea seeks refuge at the court of King Augias where she later falls in love with Heracles cleaning out the king's stables. (F)

13. Euripides explores the idea that if the good can suffer unjustly, then the wicked may also prosper. (T)

14. The public, male attitude toward women in Athens at the time of Euripides mirrors that of Jason toward Medea. (T)

15. Athens was extraordinary for its time in its view of justice and equality for women as well as for men. (F)

16. In the *Medea,* Euripides mocks the traditional tragic vision of the heroic values of ancient myth. (T)

17. After the murder of the princess, Medea receives a symbolic sanction from her goddess protector, Hecate. (F)

MULTIPLE-CHOICE QUESTIONS

18. Who was Medea's father?
    a. King Aegeus of Athens
    b. King Aeetes of Colchis (*)
    c. King Polybus of Corinth
    d. King Creon of Corinth

19. In later years, Euripides left Athens. Where did he go?
    a. Macedonia (*)
    b. Sparta
    c. Lesbos
    d. Delphi

20. Medea believes she has the support of three divine powers. Which of the following is not one of them?
    a. Hecate
    b. Themis
    c. Artemis (*)
    d. Zeus

21. What happens to Medea after her acts of violence?
    a. She goes to Athens, where King Aegeus gives her refuge. (*)
    b. She goes to Elis, where King Augias gives her refuge.
    c. She stays in Corinth, where King Creon gives her refuge.
    d. She is buried alive by King Creon, and hangs herself in the cave.

22. How does Jason die?
    a. He is struck on the head by Theseus, who was sent by King Aegeus.
    b. He is struck on the head by a beam while asleep on his ship. (*)
    c. He is murdered by Medea in his sleep.
    d. He is murdered by Medea's nurse to avenge her mistress, who has been buried alive.

23. When Medea taunts Jason with the notion that he thinks the old gods no longer prevail, what may she be referring to?
    a. that the gods are dead and the world is left without order
    b. that an older generation of chthonic gods such as Hecate have taken over (*)
    c. that Uranus was deposed by Zeus, and that Zeus soon will be deposed by a stronger son
    d. that Jason will be punished because he has lost faith

24. Why can't Medea go back to her father?
    a. because she killed him to help Jason get the Golden Fleece
    b. because she killed her brother to help Jason escape her father (*)
    c. because both he and her mother are dead, and strangers rule her homeland
    d. because she doesn't want her father to know how Jason has treated her

25. Why does Medea kill her own children?
    a. She is planning to commit suicide and doesn't trust anyone else to care for them.
    b. They are her adopted children by Jason's first marriage, and she wants to hurt Jason.
    c. She wants to hurt Jason. (*)
    d. She has developed an extreme sensitivity to the noise of children.

ESSAY QUESTIONS

26. Compare Medea and Clytemnestra as heroines; what do they have in common? What do their different fates reveal about the moral viewpoints of the *Agamemnon* and the *Medea*?

27. Medea has been variously described as a strong, independent woman, a woman with passion, and a witch; using specific examples from the play, discuss what view is finally conveyed.

28. In the following passage, who speaks, and what is the significance of the remark?

    > Moderation! Firstly, the very name of it is excellent; to practice it is easily the best thing for mortals. Excess avails to no good purpose for men, and if the gods are provoked, brings greater ruin on a house.

29. Do you agree with the viewpoints expressed in the following two quotes from the *Medea*? Why or why not?

    (1) Woman in most respects is a timid creature, with no heart for strife and aghast at the sight of steel; but wronged in love, there is no heart more murderous than hers.
    (2) You women have actually come to believe that, lucky in love, you are lucky in all things, but let some mischance befall that love, and you will think the best of all possible worlds a most loathsome place. There ought to have been some other way for men to beget their children, dispensing with the assistance of women. Then there would be no trouble in the world.

CHAPTER 18

TRIUMPH OF THE IRRATIONAL: EURIPIDES'S *BACCHANTS*

TRUE/FALSE QUESTIONS

1. Euripides's *Bacchants* was written about fifty-two years before Aeschylus's *Oresteia.* (F)

2. King Pentheus is the twin brother of Dionysus. (F)

3. King Pentheus's mother was the sister of Dionysus's mother. (T)

4. Euripides wrote the *Bacchants* in Macedonia where he witnessed the cult's rituals in the wild. (T)

5. Athenian civilization was deteriorating due to the war with Persia. (F)

6. The *Bacchants* is named for its two choruses, Asian female devotees of Dionysus and Theban women of the Dionysus cult. (T)

7. Pentheus's father had sprung from the tooth of a dragon. (T)

8. Dionysus appears to Pentheus as a young effeminate stranger, and Pentheus does not recognize him. (T)

9. Agave kills her son and carries off his severed head, believing that she is carrying the head of a bear. (F)

10. *Anagnorisis* means recollection. (F)

11. Dionysus transforms Pentheus into a Tiresias lookalike as part of the disguise. (F)

12. The play reveals that Pentheus suffers from anxiety about his sexual identity. (T)

13. Pentheus is torn to pieces by his mother. (T)

14. Tiresias accepts the divinity of Dionysus because he has given wine to humanity. (T)

15. Tiresias is summoned from the dead to give Pentheus advice about Dionysus which he does not heed. (F)

16. Tiresias understood Pentheus's sexual problems, himself being half-man and half-woman. (F)

17. Dionysus punishes Cadmus, the founder of Thebes, by turning him into a boar. (T)

18. The text states that Dionysus is incapable of feeling pity for humans, since sympathy is a human feeling. (T)

19. Agave takes her own life because she has killed her son. (F)

20. Delphi had a shrine for Dionysus as well as the oracle of Apollo. (T)

MULTIPLE-CHOICE QUESTIONS

21. What was the kinship between Pentheus and Dionysus?
    a. They were twin brothers.
    b. Their mothers were sisters. (*)
    c. Their fathers were brothers.
    d. They had the same mother; Pentheus's father was mortal, while Dionysus's father was Zeus.

22. What does *anagnorisis* mean?
    a. recognition (*)
    b. recollection
    c. reconstitution
    d. reversal

23. Which of the following is a similarity between Agave and Cassandra?
    a. They both refuse to take part in the sacrificial sparagmos.
    b. They both refuse to submit completely to a god. (*)
    c. They both refuse to take part in the sacred hieros gamos.
    d. They both become impregnated by a god.

24. Cadmus's punishment by Dionysus carries an element of irony. Why?
    a. because he is turned into a boar, and he had a reputation as a boar-killer
    b. because he is turned into a woman, and he had a reputation as antifeminine
    c. because he is turned into a snake, and he had a reputation as a dragon-killer (*)
    d. because he is sent to the Underworld, and he had boasted that he was immortal

25. Why was Tiresias able to reconcile the opposites of control and freedom?
    a. because he was used to reconciling opposites due to the fact that he was half-human, half-divine
    b. because he was used to reconciling opposites due to the fact that he was half-human, half-horse
    c. because he was used to reconciling opposites due to the fact that he was half-man, half-woman
    d. because he was used to reconciling opposites due to the fact that he once had been changed into a woman and then back into a man (*)

26. Who is Lord Bromius?
    a. Tiresias
    b. Dionysus (*)
    c. Zeus
    d. Apollo

ESSAY QUESTIONS

27. Explain and comment on the following passage, and identify the speaker:

> Mankind, young man, has two chief blessings: goddess Demeter—the earth, that is; call her whichever name you will—who sustains men with solid food, and this son of Semele, who came later and matched her gift. He invented the liquid draught of the grape and introduced it to mortals. When they get their fill of the flowing grape, it stops their grief. It gives them sleep and forgetfulness of daily sorrows. There is no other medicine for trouble. The libations we pour are the god himself making our peace with the gods, so that through him mankind may obtain blessings.

28. Why does Pentheus refuse Tiresias's advice to welcome the new deity? What is suggested by the fact that Dionysus and Pentheus are first cousins?

29. Can the opposing forces in the *Bacchants* be understood more clearly through a structuralist interpretation? Explain why or why not.

30. Compare the myth of the god's return with the account of Jesus's rejection by his family and former neighbors in Mark, chapter 6, and Luke, chapter 4.

CHAPTER 19
PLATO'S USE OF MYTHOLOGY

TRUE/FALSE QUESTIONS

1. The wars between Athens and Sparta inspired the Greeks to choose the rational practice of moderation over emotional excesses. (F)

2. The Oracle at Delphi pronounced that no one in Greece was wiser than Socrates and Euripides. (T)

3. Socrates was executed by the city of Athens for asking questions about values most Athenians took for granted. (T)

4. Socrates made his favorite student, Plato, the chief speaker in most of his dialogues. (F)

5. For Plato the world we see around us is not true reality; true reality can't be seen with our eyes. (T)

6. For Plato, true reality is the world of change; whatever does not change is not truly real. (F)

7. Plato is considered one of the great preservers and reinterpreters of Homeric myth. (F)

8. The "Allegory of the Cave" illustrates the soul's earthly imprisonment; we are like prisoners in a cave who mistake shadows for realities. (T)

9. The "Myth of Er" illustrates the soul's fate after death; after Er is killed in battle, his soul travels to the Underworld where he sees Sisyphus, Tantalus, and others being tormented. (F)

10. In the final end, Er realizes that there is no free choice; the gods have determined everything, including his next reincarnation. (F)

11. There are elements of the cult of Orpheus in Plato's "Myth of Er." (T)

12. The Platonic split between physical and spiritual reality greatly inspired early Christianity. (T)

13. In the dialogue the *Symposium,* Plato gives us an account of how he believes the sexes originated. (F)

14. In the dialogue the *Symposium,* Plato lets Aristophanes give a humorous account of the origin of the sexes. (T)

15. In the dialogue the *Symposium,* we hear that there once were three sexes: one male, one female, and one neuter. (F)

16. One of our key sources of the story of Atlantis is Plato. (T)

17. In the "Allegory of the Cave," the philosopher who escapes the cave is free to explore true reality from then on. (F)

18. In the "Myth of Er," the souls who are judged good ascend to heaven, to spend eternity there. (F)

19. Odysseus chooses his next reincarnation to be that of a swan. (F)

20. In his next life, Agamemnon chose to be a sailor so that he would not have to marry again. (F)

MULTIPLE-CHOICE QUESTIONS

21. What does the Socratic method involve?
    a. exploring the depths of human emotions
    b. questioning values that many others take for granted (*)
    c. organizing armed opposition to the government
    d. abstaining from engaging in the world of politics

22. How do we know about Socrates's philosophy?
    a. through Plato's writings (*)
    b. through Socrates's own writings
    c. through the plays of Sophocles
    d. through the plays of Euripides

23. In the "Myth of Er," there are elements of three cults except which one of the following?
    a. the cult of Dionysus
    b. the cult of Heracles (*)
    c. the cult of Demeter
    d. the cult of Orpheus

24. Virgil's *Aeneid* uses which element from the writings of Plato?
    a. the superiority of spiritual reality to physical reality (*)
    b. the myth of Atlantis
    c. the etiological myth of the origin of the sexes
    d. the criticism of Homeric myth as undignified

25. Judeo-Christian beliefs about the afterlife are anticipated by which Platonic literary feature?
    a. the "Allegory of the Cave"
    b. the "Myth of Er" (*)
    c. the story of Atlantis
    d. the origin of the sexes

26. Which of the following was NOT one of the three sexes mentioned in the dialogue the *Symposium?*
    a. male
    b. neuter (*)
    c. female
    d. androgynous

27. What kind of reincarnation does Odysseus choose for himself in the "Myth of Er"?
    a. a swan
    b. an eagle
    c. an ordinary man (*)
    d. a blind seer

ESSAY QUESTIONS

28. Explain why Plato's view of philosophy can be described as "Apollonian."

29. Describe the myth of the origin of the sexes, and explain why it can be described as etiological.

30. Explain the following passage in terms of Plato's dualism of matter and spirit, and find a modern equivalent of the allegory:

> Imagine the condition of men living in a sort of cavernous chamber underground, with an entrance open to the light and a long passage all down the cave. Here they have been from childhood, chained by the leg and also by the neck, so that they cannot move and can see only what is in front of them, because the chains will not let them turn their heads. At some distance higher up is the light of a fire burning behind them; and between the prisoners and the fire is a track with a parapet built along it, like the screen at a puppet-show, which hides the performers while they show their puppets over the top. . . . In the first place prisoners so confined would have seen nothing of themselves or of one another, except the shadows thrown by the firelight on the wall of the Cave facing them, would they?

CHAPTER 20

THE ROMAN VISION:
GREEK MYTHS AND ROMAN REALITIES

TRUE/FALSE QUESTIONS

1. Roman mythology has borrowed elements from the Etruscan culture. (T)

2. The Romans, feeling culturally inferior to the Etruscans, adopted Etruscan literature and mythology, while changing names and adapting the concepts to fit their ideas and values. (F)

3. According to the myth of Romulus and Remus, Rhea Silvia was raped by her uncle Amulius, thus conceiving the twins. (F)

4. According to Plutarch, the myth of Romulus and Remus implies that Rhea Silvia was raped by her uncle. (T)

5. Romulus and Remus were set adrift on the river Tiber and nursed by a sea-wolf. (F)

6. The twins quarreled, and Remus was killed. Rome was later named in his honor. (F)

7. Romulus's followers acquired women by sending messengers to neighboring cities and inviting the daughters of prominent citizens to become Roman wives. (F)

8. The Romans invited the Lapiths to their banquet and proceeded to abduct and rape the Lapith women. (F)

9. Contrary to Greek mythology, Roman mythology is teleological. (T)

10. Roman myth has fewer fantastic components than Greek myth. (T)

11. The poet Horace reinterprets Zeus's appearance to Danae as a shower of gold as an image of bribery. (T)

12. Romulus's ancestor is Aeneas, the Greek hero of the battle of Troy. (F)

13. One of the major Roman deities is Ceres, the Roman version of Demeter. (T)

14. An important group of spirits in the Roman household were the Pinatas. (F)

15. The Lares were guardian spirits of the home. (T)

16. In Rome patriotism was a civic virtue; if someone defied the gods, it was tantamount to committing treason. (T)

17. Three early Roman qualities are essential: gravitas, pietas, and veritas. (F)

18. Duty requires the Roman hero to control his desires for the greater good of Eternal Rome. (T)

MULTIPLE-CHOICE QUESTIONS

19. Who gave birth to Romulus and Remus?
    a. a she-wolf
    b. a sea-wolf
    c. Rhea Silvia (*)
    d. Juno

20. From where did Romulus get his army of men?
    a. They grew from dragon's teeth that he had sowed in a field.
    b. They were disgruntled farmers and runaway slaves from the region. (*)
    c. They were recruited from the Sabines.
    d. They were descendants of the Trojans in northern Italy.

21. What Roman personality traces his ancestry to Aeneas's son?
    a. Julius Caesar (*)
    b. Horace
    c. Cicero
    d. Virgil

22. Three gods were the public counterparts of the three household spirits. Which was NOT one of these gods?
    a. Jupiter
    b. Minerva (*)
    c. Juno
    d. Ceres

23. What is meant by the statement that mythology is teleological?
    a. It is goal-oriented. (*)
    b. It focuses on divine powers.
    c. It is less than logical.
    d. It is a remnant of a very ancient tradition.

24. What does it mean for myths to have a didactic function? Choose the most precise definition.
    a. They function as a political charter.
    b. They are not supposed to be taken seriously: a comic relief.
    c. They are intended to teach a lesson. (*)
    d. They are stories about feminine powers.

25. Which was NOT one of the three types of deities in the Roman household?
    a. the Penates
    b. the Vesta
    c. the Lares
    d. the Mores (*)

26. Three early Roman qualities were essential; which one wasn't?
    a. gravitas
    b. geritas (*)
    c. pietas
    d. frugalitas

ESSAY QUESTIONS

27. Explain in detail how Roman mythology has a charter function.

28. Describe at least two ways in which the Romans transformed Greek myths.

29. Contrast the rape of the Sabine women with the Greek myth in which the centaurs attempted to rape the Lapith women, and explain how these two myths differ in terms of the female perspective in Greek and Roman culture.

30. Explain how the Roman hero differs from his Greek counterparts.

CHAPTER 21

THE *AENEID:* VIRGIL'S ROMAN EPIC

TRUE/FALSE QUESTIONS

1. Because of his experiences during the Trojan War, Virgil became a supporter of the Roman Empire. (F)

2. Virgil's works include the *Aeneid* and several poems eulogizing the glory of war. (F)

3. Virgil ordered his manuscript to be destroyed upon his death, but the Emperor Augustus saved it from destruction. (T)

4. Like all other Roman literature at the time, the *Aeneid* was written in Greek. (F)

5. The first six books of the *Aeneid* are modeled on the *Odyssey*; the rest is modeled on the *Iliad.* (T)

6. The narration of the *Aeneid* includes the founding of Rome by Aeneas. (F)

7. Dido was Aeneas's second wife. (F)

8. The residents of the lands surrounding Rome generally resented the Roman conquerors as imperialist aggressors. (F)

9. In the end, Aeneas is rewarded by being taken to Rome by his mother, Venus. (F)

10. While Achilles and Odysseus had a choice of fates, Aeneas must do as the gods have predetermined. (T)

11. The expression "to have a monkey on one's back" originated with the *Aeneid* where Aeneas, in the opening sequence, carried the sacred household monkey on his back when leaving Troy. (F)

12. Aeneas displays righteous indignation when Turnus, after having killed Aeneas's young lover in battle, boasts of the kill by wearing the young man's belt. (T)

13. The fact that Creusa appears as a shade to Aeneas is an image of her insubstantial value. (T)

14. One of the pro-Roman female characters of the *Aeneid* is Venus. (T)

15. Aeneas leaves Juno, the woman he loves, to marry Creusa, because he is ordered to do so by Mercury. (F)

16. In the Underworld, Aeneas learns the meaning of his suffering from the shade of his father, Anchises. (T)

17. The climax of the *Aeneid*, the combat between Turnus and Aeneas, parallels the combat between Hector and Achilles. (T)

18. Differences between the *Iliad* and the *Aeneid* include the characters of Patrocles and Pallas; Patrocles was an inexperienced youth in his first battle, whereas Pallas was an experienced fighter. (F)

19. Some scholars claim that Virgil's representation of "Rome triumphant" is actually ironic. (T)

20. Part of Virgil's description of the Underworld is borrowed from a dialogue by Plato. (T)

MULTIPLE-CHOICE QUESTIONS

21. Who was Aeneas's second wife?
    a. Dido
    b. Creusa
    c. Dodo
    d. Lavinia (*)

22. The text mentions four aspects of the governing role of the city. Which is NOT one of those four aspects?
    a. to create good conditions for civilized life
    b. to establish good government
    c. to erect buildings and monuments
    d. to raise taxes to pay for itself (*)

23. Who is the real hero of the *Aeneid*?
    a. Turnus
    b. Troy
    c. Aeneas
    d. Rome (*)

24. What did Aeneas carry on his back when leaving Troy?
    a. his wife
    b. his father (*)
    c. his son
    d. a monkey

25. What reward did Aeneas receive during his lifetime for furthering the gods' plans for Rome?
    a. Nothing. (*)
    b. He was shown a vision of Rome of the future.
    c. He was taken to Rome by his mother, Venus.
    d. He was reunited with Dido.

26. Under what conditions did Turnus kill Pallas?
    a. in a fit of jealousy
    b. in battle (*)
    c. by accident, during a fist fight
    d. He mistook him for Aeneas.

27. Who becomes Aeneas's moral guide in the Underworld?
    a. his friend, Hector
    b. his mother, Creusa
    c. his father, Anchises (*)
    d. his lover, Pallas

ESSAY QUESTIONS

28. In what specific ways is the *Aeneid* like the *Iliad* and the *Odyssey*? Why does Virgil want to remind us of these similarities?

29. Why does Aeneas go to the Underworld, and what does he learn there?

30. Describe some of the ways in which myth and real history intersect in the *Aeneid*.

31. Identify the speaker and explain the following passage; then compare it with Plato's "Myth of Er."

    First each of us must suffer his own Shade;
    then we are sent through wide Elysium—
    a few of us will gain the Fields of Gladness—
    until the finished cycle of the ages,
    with lapse of days, annuls the ancient stain
    and leaves the power of ether pure in us,
    the fire of spirit simple and unsoiled.
    But all the rest, when they have passed time's circle
    for a millennium, are summoned by
    the god to Lethe in a great assembly
    that, free of memory, they may return
    beneath the curve of the upper world, that they
    may once again begin to wish for bodies.

32. Interpret Jupiter and Juno's conversation in book 12 in terms of a charter function.

CHAPTER 22
OVID'S *METAMORPHOSES:*
THE RETELLING OF GREEK MYTHS

TRUE/FALSE QUESTIONS

1. Ovid had to spend the last decade of his life in exile because he was banished from Rome by Augustus. (T)

2. Ovid's theme in *Metamorphoses* is "bodies changed." (T)

3. One possible reason why Augustus banished Ovid was his portrayal of the emperor as Cerberus, the hound from Hell. (F)

4. Ovid satirized Augustus's attempt at imposing moral restraints on the Roman upper class. (T)

5. Ovid regarded a return to chaos as the only possible solution to Rome's problems of imperial tyranny. (F)

6. Ovid commonly criticized the gods for turning humans into inanimate things such as trees, rocks, and constellations, just before the fulfillment of their accomplishments. (F)

7. Perseus turns all of Andromeda's suitors to stone one by one by showing them the Gorgon's head. (F)

8. Daphne's only way to escape from Apollo is to be dehumanized. (T)

9. Ovid implies in *Metamorphoses* that his own fame will eclipse Caesar's. (T)

MULTIPLE-CHOICE QUESTIONS

10. What is the main theme in *Metamorphoses*?
    a. "immortal souls"
    b. "bodies changed" (*)
    c. "might makes right"
    d. "reincarnation"

11. With whom does Ovid equate Augustus?
    a. Jupiter (*)
    b. Pluto
    c. Cerberus
    d. the Gorgon

12. Romans were caught between the terror of anarchy and the threat of
    a. chaos.
    b. law. (*)
    c. the gods.
    d. history.

13. Why does the text claim that Ovid's story of Perseus is a "Roman petrification of Greek myth"?
    a. because Perseus kills Andromeda's suitors with a sword of stone
    b. because Perseus kills Andromeda's suitors by turning them into stone, one at a time
    c. because Perseus kills Andromeda's suitors by turning them into stone, all at once (*)
    d. because Andromeda flees Perseus and is turned into stone

14. Ovid makes it clear that the Romans had a compulsive need for
    a. change.
    b. chaos.
    c. a tyrant ruler.
    d. permanence and order. (*)

15. The metamorphosis of Daphne into a laurel tree can be viewed as
    a. an etiological myth. (*)
    b. a charter myth.
    c. a rite of passage.
    d. an example of Euhemerism.

16. Which event is marked by the following happenings, described by Ovid?

    In the market place,
    Around the homes of men and the gods' temples
    Dogs howled by night, and the shadows of the silent
    Went roaming, and great earthquakes shook the city.

    a. the impending fall of Rome
    b. the impending murder of Caesar (*)
    c. the death of Augustus, prophesied
    d. the death of Ovid himself, prophesied

ESSAY QUESTIONS

17. Compare Ovid's description of the "Ages of Man" with Hesiod's (chapter 4), and point out specifically Roman views and ideas.

18. What does Apollo want from Daphne? Why does she refuse him? What does his attempted rape suggest about the relationship between humans and gods?

19. Compare and contrast Virgil's and Ovid's views of "Eternal Rome."

CHAPTER 23
THE PERSISTENCE OF MYTH

TRUE/FALSE QUESTIONS

1. During the Dark Ages, the hero of classical mythology was considered inappropriate for a Christian focus on humility and otherworldliness. (T)

2. In the early Middle Ages, classical mythology was rediscovered through the works of Euripides and Sophocles. (F)

3. In the late Middle Ages, classical mythology was rediscovered through the works of Ovid and Virgil. (T)

4. Dante was inspired by Ovid's poems about the art of love. (T)

5. Modern advertising often uses mythic images as emblems. (T)

6. One of the four basic ways of transmitting mythic material today is to make ancient plays or poems accessible to modern readers through modern translations and performances. (T)

7. The study of Greek was revived in the Romantic Age after having been unpopular during the Renaissance. (F)

8. Even the ancient Greek playwrights wrote critical revisions of classical myths. (T)

9. Revisionism of classical mythology began in the Renaissance. (F)

10. One of the writers revising Greek myth and incorporating it in his own work is Jean-Paul Sartre. (T)

11. Jean-Paul Sartre wrote a version of *Antigone* intended as a criticism of the French Vichy government during World War II. (F)

12. Igor Stravinsky is one of the composers using mythic material in his own music. (T)

13. One of the novels mentioned which incorporate Homeric elements is Malamud's *The Natural*. (T)

14. Since myth generally takes place in a social vacuum, myths can tell us nothing about cultural changes. (F)

15. Rubens and Poussin painted different versions of the centaurs raping the Lapith women. (F)

167

16. During the Renaissance, painters for the first time were striving to depict historical figures in garments appropriate for their historical time period. (F)

17. Sir Philip Sidney's sonnets deal with the conflict between Ovidian images and Christian belief. (T)

18. For the Greeks, Icarus represented a lesson in the necessity of the Golden Mean of moderation. (T)

19. In the Renaissance, Doctor Faustus is compared with Icarus; in the Romantic period he is compared with Prometheus. (T)

20. During the Renaissance, the character of Icarus represented a lesson in the necessity of the Golden Mean of moderation. (F)

MULTIPLE-CHOICE QUESTIONS

21. Mythic material is NOT frequently transmitted in which one of these ways?
    a. by using a mythic figure as an emblem or a symbol
    b. by updating ancient stories to make them relevant to contemporary audiences
    c. by making ancient plays or poems accessible to modern readers through modern translations and performances
    d. by incorporating ancient mythic images in modern religious contexts (*)

22. In the late Middle Ages, classical mythology was rediscovered through the works of which writers?
    a. Virgil and Ovid (*)
    b. Euripides and Sophocles
    c. Dante and Petrarch
    d. Plato and Aristotle

23. Who wrote a version of *Antigone* intended as a criticism of the French Vichy government during World War II?
    a. Jean-Paul Sartre
    b. Jean Anouilh (*)
    c. Jean Giraudoux
    d. Jean Cousin the Elder

24. Who was Claude Lorrain?
    a. the first opera composer
    b. a French political playwright
    c. a French painter (*)
    d. a French poet

25. Which one of the following novels is NOT specifically mentioned in the text as using extended mythic themes?
    a. John Updike's *The Centaur*
    b. Victor Hugo's *Les Miserables* (*)
    c. James Joyce's *Portrait of the Artist as a Young Man*
    d. Bernard Malamud's *The Natural*

26. Many modern ecologists make use of which classical figure in Greek mythology as their symbol?
    a. Athene
    b. Cronus
    c. Poseidon
    d. Gaea (*)

27. Which one of the following interpretations of the story of Orpheus and Eurydice is NOT mentioned in the text?
    a. The story symbolizes a grand but tragic passion.
    b. The story symbolizes a descent into existential despair.
    c. The story symbolizes a descent into the depths of the human psyche.
    d. The story symbolizes the soul reaching toward God and eternity. (*)

28. Which event in classical mythology did both Rubens and Poussin paint?
    a. the rape of the Sabine women (*)
    b. the rape of the Lapith women
    c. the fall of Icarus
    d. Prometheus chained to the rock

29. For the Greeks, Icarus represented a certain moral lesson. Which one?
    a. a lesson of the audacious spirit breaking through the limits of conventions
    b. a lesson in the necessity of the Golden Mean of moderation (*)
    c. a lesson in the indifference of the gods to human suffering
    d. a lesson in human civic duty

30. Which historical personality of the early nineteenth century was compared to Prometheus?
    a. Beethoven
    b. Dr. Frankenstein
    c. Napoleon (*)
    d. Lord Byron

ESSAY QUESTIONS

31. Explain what is meant by the statement that Icarus is the heroic symbol for the Renaissance.

32. Speculate how feminist psychologists may be using the images of Athene, Artemis, and Aphrodite in their analysis of female nature.

33. Identify the author and the theme of the following passage, and explain what it means:

> To suffer woes which Hope thinks infinite;
> To forgive wrongs darker than death or night;
> To defy Power, which seems omnipotent;
> To live, and bear; to hope till Hope creates
> From its own wreck the thing it contemplates;
> Neither to change, nor falter, nor repent;
> This, like thy glory, Titan, is to be
> Good, great and joyous, beautiful and free;
> This alone is Life, Joy, Empire, and Victory.

34. Compare W. H. Auden's "The Shield of Achilles" with the corresponding chapter in the *Iliad*; how do the differences reflect ancient versus modern beliefs or values?